ADVENTURES WITH INSECTS

ADVENTURES WITH INSECTS

Richard Headstrom

Illustrated by the Author

DOVER PUBLICATIONS, INC.
NEW YORK

Published in Canada by General Publishing Company, Ltd.,
30 Lesmill Road, Don Mills, Toronto, Ontario.
Published in the United Kingdom by Constable and Company, Ltd., 10 Orange Street, London WC2H 7EG.

This Dover edition, first published in 1982, is an unabridged
republication of the work originally published in 1963 by J. B.
Lippincott Company, Philadelphia. The listing of biological
supply houses has been brought up to date.

Manufactured in the United States of America
Dover Publications, Inc.
180 Varick Street
New York, N.Y. 10014

Library of Congress Cataloging in Publication Data

Headstrom, Richard, 1902-
    Adventures with insects.

    Originally published: 1st ed. Philadelphia : Lippincott, 1963.
    Summary: Thirty-nine adventures in which the anatomy, be-
havior, and social life of insects are described.
    1. Insects—Juvenile literature. [1. Insects]
I. Title.
QL467.H4   1982   595.7   82-7451
ISBN 0-486-21955-0 (pbk.)   AACR2

TO MY WIFE

For Her Patience and Understanding

CONTENTS

IT IS GENERALLY believed that somewhere between 625,000 and 1,250,000 different kinds of insects have been named and described. No one knows the exact number because there are so many different species it is impossible to keep count of them all. And these appear to be only a fraction of the total number that are presumed to exist. Some believe there may be as many as 2,000,000; others as many as 10,000,000. From the viewpoint of species alone the number is staggering, and if we should multiply the minimum number of species by the total possible individuals of each species we would arrive at a fantastic figure.

Aside from the vast numbers, which in itself is enough to stimulate anyone's imagination, consider further that the habits of no two species are identical and that each reveals some difference in food, structure, or habit. We know a great deal about insects and much has been written about them, but the sum of our knowledge is but a fraction of what remains to be learned. Of the minimum number of insects described it is doubtful if the immature forms of 10,000 are known, and this is only one aspect of the subject. Indeed the science of entomology is so vast in scope that no professional entomologist can hope to be thoroughly acquainted with it. It is a study in which something new can always be discovered. Today space travel, atomic energy, electronics, and the like may have more glamorous appeal to the boy and girl entering the study of science, and insects may seem of trifling account—but bear in mind that they pose a greater threat to man's continued existence and survival in this world than any other enemy, real or fancied.

Apart from this threat insects can provide much in the way of enjoyment and pleasure. To become acquainted with them and to learn about them is not so much a study but an adventure—or, shall we say, a series of adventures. For a person with an inquiring mind, with an eager desire to learn, and with an interest in the outdoors, they offer a fascinating hobby and provide a challenge to add to our knowledge. And one doesn't need a doctor's degree or expensive equipment or a bent for mathematics—as a matter of fact, much of what we know about insects has been contributed by people who were not professional entomologists, but people in all walks of life who found in the study of insects a gratifying way of spending their hours of leisure. The study of insects is a hobby that can be rewarding in many ways. If you are not too sure of what I mean, perhaps you will find out by coming with me on the following adventures.

HAVE YOU ever seen an egg that looks like a tiny flowerpot? Or one that resembles a miniature golf ball? Or one that has a circle of spines?

Most of us think of eggs in terms of those we had for breakfast. Few of us ever see any others except in the spring, when we occasionally find a blue robin's egg on the ground or look into a nest to which we have easy access. Perhaps we may even pass a pond or spring pool when the frogs and toads are mating and find their eggs in floating masses. But except for such instances our experience with eggs is usually confined to the kind we use for food.

Should we go outdoors and poke about with a discerning eye, we would find eggs of all shapes and colors and some that are beautifully ornamented or exquisitely sculptured. And it doesn't matter what time of the year, although our efforts would be best rewarded in spring and summer. Even in the midst of winter we can find eggs attached to twigs and branches, or clustered to tree trunks and fences, or hidden away in cracks and crevices. Do you want to see an egg that looks like a tiny flowerpot? Select a day in winter and go out and look on the branches of almost any tree. You should find not one, but hundreds of them (Figure 1). These are the eggs of the fall cankerworm. Don't let the word "worm" mislead you, for they were not

11

We Look for Eggs and Are Surprised at What We Find

Figure 1
EGG OF FALL CANKERWORM

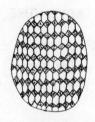

laid by a worm but by a wingless moth.

Where can you find an egg that resembles a miniature golf ball? In any vegetable garden during the summer where beets, spinach, or chard are grown, for the eggs are laid by a small fly—the spinach-leaf miner—on these plants (Figure 2). For the egg that has a circle of spines, you will have to do more searching. There is such an egg (Figure 3) and it is laid on various plants in fields and meadows by an insect opprobriously called the stinkbug. It is a name well taken, but more fastidious people would rather have it called the shield bug, a name also well taken. If you are not successful in finding this egg, perhaps you will settle for the egg of a related species called the harlequin cabbage bug. The egg resembles a small barrel (Figure 4). It is white with two black bands and a white spot and is easier to find, since it is laid on the leaves of cabbage, potato, eggplant, and radish, any one of which is likely to be found in a vegetable garden.

By now you know that we are talking about insect eggs. Contrary to a popular misconception, most insect eggs can be seen with the naked eye, though there are some that tax our vision. One of the smallest is that of the clover-seed midge. It measures about .30 millimeter in length. When you go in search of insect eggs, I would suggest you take along a magnifying glass so you can observe them to

12

the best advantage, especially such eggs as those of the milkweed and white cabbage butterflies. With your glass you will find that they are ribbed and not smooth, as we would expect eggs to be (Figure 5).

Once you have looked at a few insect eggs, they will prove a lure to you to look for others, for insect eggs show such diversity in form and color and in many other respects that almost every kind will have something to offer. Take color, for instance. Almost every color and color combination imaginable is represented. There are the brown eggs of the squash bug, the dark-green eggs of the twelve-spotted asparagus beetle, and the pale-yellow eggs of the white cabbage butterfly. Then we have the red eggs of the chinch bug, the chalky white eggs of the beet-leaf miner, the orange eggs of the bean-leaf beetle, the pink eggs of the lesser cornstalk borer, and the black eggs of the corn-root aphid.

Insect eggs can be anything but egg-shaped. The eggs of swallowtail butterflies are spherical (Figure 6); those of tree crickets, long and curved (Figure 7). Assassin bugs lay eggs that are usually cylindrical (Figure 8). Would you expect an egg to be flat? Then go out and look for the eggs of the codling moth. Unfortunately you can find them only from the time when the apple blossoms begin to appear until the petals begin to fall. Even then they are difficult to find, for they are flat and scale-

Figure 5
EGG OF WHITE CABBAGE BUTTERFLY

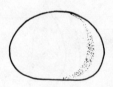

Figure 6
EGG OF SWALLOWTAIL BUTTERFLY

Figure 7
EGG OF TREE CRICKET

Figure 8
EGG OF ASSASSIN BUG

Figure 9
EGGS OF CODLING MOTH

Figure 10
EGG OF STONE FLY

like and so extremely thin and transparent that they are barely visible, and then only by reflected light (Figure 9).

We have already mentioned the eggs of the stinkbugs with their circle of spines. The eggs of stone flies have a cap which is often ornamented with raylike extensions (Figure 10), and the eggs of water scorpions are furnished with long filaments. *Ranatra* (Figure 11) has two, *Nepa* three. The egg of the poultry louse is white and covered with glasslike spines, and at one end has a lid which bears at its apex a long, lashlike whip (Figure 12).

There doesn't seem to be much method in regard to the manner in which eggs are laid. Some are deposited singly (Figure 13), others in rows (Figure 14), others on top of one another (Figure 15). Some are laid in clusters which are covered with a varnishlike coating (Figure 16), some in masses overlaid with a hard covering of silk (Figure 17). Others are covered with hairs from the female's body (Figure 18), and still others with a waxy coating (Figure 19). Indeed eggs are covered with all sorts of materials, including fecula and regurgitated food. To what purpose? One, to protect them against winter conditions; another, to make them less conspicuous to enemies.

Some years ago an entomologist said that no collection of insects is complete without specimens of the eggs. That is true. If you

14

Figure 11
EGG OF WATER SCORPION

Figure 12
EGG OF POULTRY LOUSE

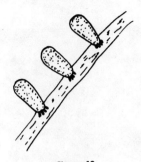

Figure 13
EGGS OF ASPARAGUS BEETLE

Figure 14
EGGS OF SQUASH BUG

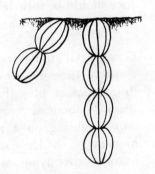

Figure 15
EGGS OF THE HOP MERCHANT

Figure 16
EGGS OF THE TENT CATERPILLAR

Figure 17
EGG MASS OF PRAYING
MANTIS

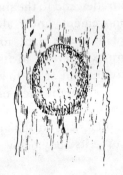

Figure 18
EGG MASS OF GYPSY MOTH

Figure 19
FEMALE ROSE SCALE EGGS
BENEATH WAX SCALE

want to prepare the life histories of various insects, bear in mind that the eggs represent the initial stage and are as much a part of the life history as any other stage. You may want to prepare a collection of eggs only to show the many different shapes and colors and other variations. The eggs may be kept in small vials, preferably with screw caps, which can be purchased in any drugstore, or they may be simply gummed to cards. Of course they should be fully labeled.

ADVENTURE 2

We Watch Some Insects Lay Their Eggs and Learn of Some Strange Habits

COME WITH ME to a pond, stream or lake on a sunny June day where we can watch the dragonflies at play (Figure 20). We watch them fly about, darting here and there, perhaps alighting on a water plant to rest a moment or suddenly streaking off in pursuit of some other flying insect. Perhaps we might see a dragonfly skim the surface of the water and then suddenly swoop down and touch it. Or we might see one of them, poised in the air, descend to the surface with a swift, curved movement, hover above the submerged leaf of a water plant for a moment, and then quickly return to its original position, only to descend again toward the submerged leaf. Or we might even observe a third dragonfly alight on the stem of an emergent water plant rather near to the surface of the water and curve its body below it.

These three dragonflies are laying eggs. Remember what I said in the Introduction —that no two species of insects have precisely the same habits? Here is a case in point for each dragonfly follows her own behavioral pattern.

In our last adventure we found that eggs may be found in all conceivable places. Do not think for a moment that the eggs are laid at random, that they are laid wherever the female happens to be when it comes time for

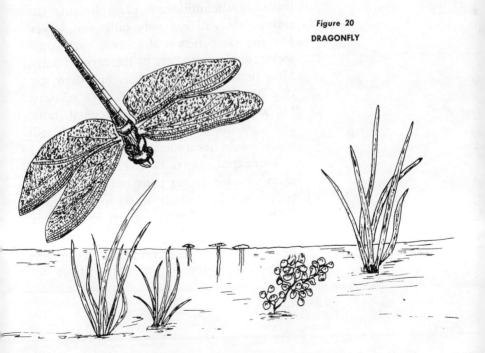

Figure 20
DRAGONFLY

her to release the eggs from her body. She lays them where she is reasonably sure that her young will have an ample supply of food when they emerge from the eggs. Thus dragonflies, whose young live in the water, deposit their eggs where the young, upon emerging from the eggs, find themselves in a habitat to which they are adapted and where food is readily available. Even the dragonflies we see flying over the fields return to the water to lay their eggs.

The eggs of the tent caterpillar are clustered on the twigs and branches of wild cherry trees because when the caterpillars emerge, they have access to fresh cherry leaves. The milkweed butterfly lays her eggs on the leaves of the milkweed plant because the caterpillars will eat only milkweed leaves. For the same reason the black swallowtail seeks out the members of the carrot family. How these insects and others find their specific host plants is something of a mystery. Of course the senses of touch, smell, taste, and sight are all involved, but there is still much we do not understand.

Terrestrial insects as a rule do not have much trouble laying their eggs where their young will have ready access to food, since both they and their young live in the same kind of environment. But what about the insects that as adults live more or less on land and whose young live in water? They are faced with the problem of getting their eggs into a habitat which, as winged insects, they are not well adapted to enter.

The problem has been solved in various ways. Some species of mosquitoes lay their eggs in dry situations where they remain until rains or melting snows provide the necessary moisture. The horseflies, dobson flies, alder flies, and certain caddis flies lay their eggs upon the branches of trees or upon stones that overhang the water or on emergent water plants, so all the young have to do when they emerge is to drop into the water. Others, as the net-veined midges, whose young cling to stones in the rapids of mountain streams, in the waters of ravines, and in rushing brooklets, lay them along the edge of the water, and it is up to the young to make their own way to the rocks and stones.

The black flies (Figure 21), whose young live in similar places, appear a little more courageous when it comes to venturing near the water, for they attach their eggs directly to the stones. Perhaps we should not give them credit for too much bravery, for they do not actually enter the water but dart at the stones as the water sprays over them. Find a rushing stream with rocks on the bottom in early May or when the weather has begun to warm up in the spring and you can see them yourself. If the water is shallow and not too swift, you may find that instead of flying

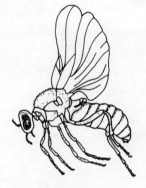

Figure 21
BLACK FLY

19

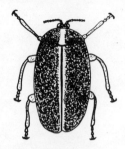

Figure 22
RIFFLE BEETLE

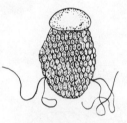

Figure 23
MAY FLY EGG WITH THREADS

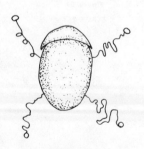

Figure 24
MAY FLY EGG WITH FLOATS

about and then darting down upon the rocks, the flies will crawl about on the surface of the rocks and then deposit their eggs.

The riffle beetles (Figure 22) also lay their eggs directly on stones in swiftly flowing streams, but they have contrived a rather ingenious way of doing so. They are covered with silken hairs which hold a film of air. On hot days the females settle on stones projecting above the water and then, enveloped in air, climb down over the water-washed stones and lay their eggs in the swiftest part of the stream. Certain May flies have copied the idea, or perhaps the beetles got it from the May flies; however, the May flies use their wings instead of hairs to entrap a film of air. One species of May flies lays eggs with threads attached to them (Figure 23); another, with floats (Figure 24), so that the eggs may be suspended or float in the water.

Egg laying among the insects is not a simple matter. As a matter of fact, the urge is so strong to safeguard the eggs and make ample provision for the young that many insects have developed unusual habits to ensure their survival. Consider the lacewing, or golden eyes. If you find a female laying her eggs, watch her by all means. From the tip of her body she ejects a drop of sticky fluid on the surface of a leaf. Then she lifts up her abdomen and spins the drop into a thread half an inch or more long which hardens almost im-

20

mediately on exposure to the air. She next lays an oblong egg about the size of a pin point on the tip of the stalk. The egg firmly in place, she spins another thread or stalk on which she lays another egg. She repeats the performance until she has laid her full complement (Figure 25). Why does she go to all this trouble? Because her young are carnivorous and feed on other insects, especially aphids. Therefore the eggs are usually laid in a colony of aphids. But eggs are also tempting. If the eggs were laid in a cluster or group, the first aphis lion, as the young are called, to emerge would very likely find the other eggs quite to its taste and eat them. Instead of having half a dozen or so offspring, the mother lacewing would have only one. So she places the eggs beyond reach. Of course there is nothing to prevent the first aphis lion from climbing the stalks, but this would be too much work when soft, juicy aphids are right at hand.

We have seen that eggs may be found in all sorts of places. Many of them were attached to branches, tree trunks, fences and the like. Didn't you wonder how they remained in place, even though buffeted by rain, wind, sleet and snow? Eggs deposited in such places are laid with a viscous substance which, upon drying, forms a cement that holds them firmly in place. But not all insects lay eggs this way. As a matter of fact, many insects lay eggs in

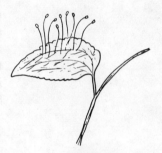

Figure 25
EGGS OF LACEWING FLY

21

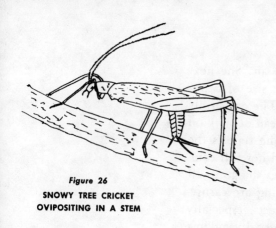

Figure 26
SNOWY TREE CRICKET
OVIPOSITING IN A STEM

places where they are completely hidden from view, as in stems (Figure 26), tree trunks, fruit, seeds, roots, and in the ground (Figure 27). They make incisions, punctures (Figure 28), scars and holes. To be able to cut the tissues of plants or to excavate holes in the soil or elsewhere they must obviously have some means of doing so. Many of them have an egg-laying device at the posterior part of the body called an ovipositor (Figure 29). It is essentially a sharp, piercing organ and may be very simple in structure or quite elaborate.

Figure 27
GRASSHOPPER OVIPOSITING
IN GROUND

Figure 28
LEAF SCARS MADE
BY BUFFALO TREE HOPPER

Figure 29
FEMALE FIELD CRICKET
SHOWING LONG OVIPOSITOR

It must be very strong, too, since it is not easy to drill a hole, say, in a tree. But the ichneumon flies (Figure 30) seem to do so rather effortlessly. They are remarkable drillers.

Once a hole has been made and eggs laid in it most insects take no further precautionary measures and simply fly away. They do not even take the trouble to attach them with cement or some other form of glue. Others, however, take certain measures to safeguard their eggs. Actually such measures are needed, for they lay their eggs in places

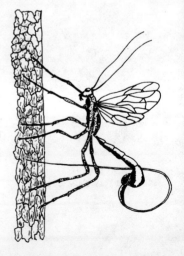

Figure 30
ICHNEUMON FLY OVIPOSITING

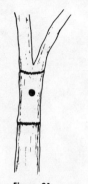

Figure 31
EGG SCAR AND GIRDLING
OF RASPBERRY-CANE BORER

Figure 32
PLUM CURCULIO

Figure 33
SCAR MADE BY PLUM CURCULIO

where they might be damaged by the growing plant. One such insect is the raspberry-cane borer. Before depositing her eggs in the new growth of raspberry cane, the female first cuts two ringlike girdles about one half inch apart around the stem a few inches below the tip. Then midway between the two rings she punctures the stem and deposits an egg (Figure 31). The two ringlike girdles cause the top of the stem to wilt and fall over and this prevents it from crushing the egg.

Some insects puncture or make incisions in plant tissues not with an ovipositor but with a prolonged beak. Such insects are generally known as snout beetles (Figure 32). One of them, the plum curculio, cuts an incision in such fruit as the plum, cherry, and peach and in the cavity thus excavated lays an egg. But she doesn't stop here. With her beak she pushes the egg to the bottom of the cavity and then cuts out a crescent-shaped slit in front of the incision and extends it obliquely beneath the cavity. The result is that the egg is left in a flap of tissue and cannot be crushed by the growing fruit (Figure 33). Remember that the raspberry-cane borer has a similar habit.

In any large group of people there is always bound to be someone different from the others. Insects aren't much different. Water bugs usually attach their eggs to water plants. But one of them has to be contrary. The fe-

24

male, unlike normal-behaving water bugs, lays her eggs on the back of the male, not infrequently with some opposition on his part, and there they remain until they hatch (Figure 34). A certain female water boatman, unlike her sisters that attach their eggs to water plants, is not satisfied to do the same but must attach her eggs to a crayfish. As we cannot understand or explain the behavior of some people, neither can we explain the behavior of these two insects.

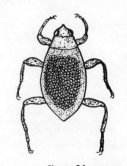

Figure 34
WATER BUG CARRYING EGGS

ALL ANIMALS HAVE TO EAT to live and insects are no exception. If you have ever seen caterpillars feeding on the leaves of a plant and seen how quickly the leaves disappear, you probably have thought that insects have voracious appetites. That is true to some extent, but insects vary in their eating habits as much as we do. There are some that are quite choosy and would rather go without than eat what does not appeal to them. And there are some, like the grasshopper, that seem to find a great deal of pleasure in eating.

During the warmer months of the year every garden, roadside, field, and meadow is a restaurant to the grasshopper, and we can find him there almost any time. Select a fairly large grasshopper. Place him in a bottle and cover the bottle with a piece of cloth so that he will not leave unexpectedly. Once he has

ADVENTURE 3

We Observe the Table Manners of Various Insects

25

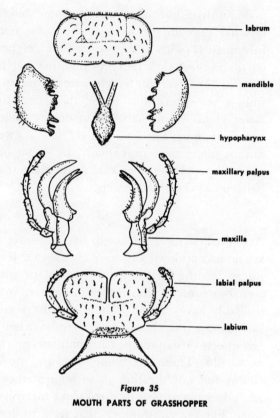

labrum

mandible

hypopharynx

maxillary palpus

maxilla

labial palpus

labium

Figure 35
MOUTH PARTS OF GRASSHOPPER

settled down, offer him a piece of crisp, juicy lettuce leaf.

As we watch the grasshopper eat at close range—we use a reading glass to do so—we are surprised to find that his upper jaws move sideways instead of up and down as we would expect. These upper jaws, or mandibles, look like a pair of nippers (Figure 35), are hard,

26

have teeth and grinding surfaces. They make most efficient biting and chewing tools. Just above the mandibles, or rather in front of them, is a flap that moves up and down. This flap is the upper lip or labrum, and the grasshopper uses it to push the pieces of leaf he bites off toward the mandibles. Below the mandibles are the lower jaws, or maxillae, and if we look at them closely we find that each is provided with an appendage called a palpus. The function of the maxillae is to hold the piece of leaf while the mandibles grind it into smaller pieces for swallowing. Directly below, or rather in front of the maxillae is the lower lip, or labium, which is also provided with a pair of palpi. The labium is used in much the same manner as the labrum. There is also a tongue, which is located on the floor of the mouth cavity and which is not quite visible. As the grasshopper eats, he constantly moves the palpi and taps the leaf with them. Sense organs of taste are located on them and help him to select his food.

If we provide him with a fresh piece of leaf, we observe that he is quite meticulous as to how he bites into it. He proceeds to devour the leaf by reaching up and cutting downward, thus making an even-edged, long hole on the leaf margin. By repeating the process he makes the hole deeper (Figure 36) or larger, and eventually the entire leaf blade is consumed.

A good many biting and chewing insects, such as caterpillars and sawfly larvae, emulate the grasshopper in eating habits. Like some people who seek a corner table in a restaurant where they may dine unobserved, some insects prefer to eat unnoticed. A certain caterpillar, *Nerice,* is dressed in a cloak of green to match the color of the leaf on which it feeds, and each segment of its body is extended upward into two points that resemble the teeth of the leaf margin (Figure 37). It prefers to dine on elm leaves, so if you want to see how cleverly it disguises itself, look for an elm tree whose leaves have been eaten along the margins.

Less fastidious insects simply dig right into

28

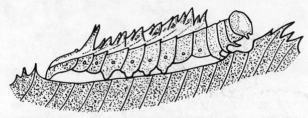

Figure 37
NERICE FEEDING ON ELM LEAF

the leaves and eat holes wherever the fancy takes them. One of these insects, the cabbage flea beetle, is very common on cruciferous plants, especially cabbage, turnip, and radish. After a few of these beetles have fed for a while, the leaves appear peppered with tiny shot holes (Figure 38). The cabbage worm also feeds in a similar manner on the same plants but makes larger holes (Figure 39). The larvae of some sawflies seemingly prefer to feed unobserved and assume an S-shaped position (Figure 40). When feeding in this

Figure 38
HOLES MADE BY
CABBAGE FLEA BEETLE

Figure 39
HOLES MADE BY CABBAGE WORM

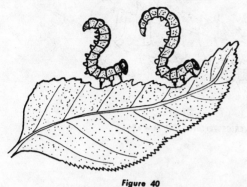

Figure 40
SAWFLY LARVAE FEEDING

Figure 41
LEAF SKELETONIZED
BY ROSE SAWFLY

manner, they are difficult to see, as they match the outlines of the holes.

A number of insects eat only the softer tissues of a leaf and leave the skeleton intact (Figure 41). They are known as skeletonizers, and you can find them everywhere. Many of the external feeders have such characteristic habits of feeding that they may often be recognized by the type of injury they inflict. We have shown three distinctive types in Figures 42, 43, and 44.

Figure 42
FEEDING HABIT OF
SAWFLY LARVAE

Figure 43
FEEDING HABIT OF
POPLAR TENTMAKER

Figure 44
FEEDING HABIT OF
TORTOISE BEETLE

IT SEEMS ALMOST INCREDIBLE that an animal should be able to peel off its skin and replace it with a new one, yet immature insects do so a number of times. All insects have an outside covering or skin, called the epidermis or cuticula, which is composed of a hard material known as chitin. This hard cuticula serves as a protective covering or sort of armor, but unfortunately it is inelastic. As a young insect eats and grows, there comes a time when the cuticula becomes too small. The insect now has two alternatives: to stop growing or to get rid of the cuticula.

Just prior to discarding the old skin, the insect forms a new skin from a liquid secreted by certain glands called hypodermal glands. This new skin is soft and elastic and can easily accommodate an increase in size. Thus when the old skin prevents any further growth, it splits open and the insect works its way out. To help it do so, a fluid which dissolves the old skin is secreted by other glands. The new skin soon becomes hardened or chitinized, and after a while it too has to be cast off. A change of skin may occur a number of times—it varies with different insects—or until the young insect has become full-grown. It then either becomes an adult insect or passes into a resting, or pupal, stage. During the pupal stage some remarkable changes transform it into an adult insect, in appearance so unlike the young insect that we could

We Watch an Unusual Process and Make Some Observations

not be blamed if we failed to recognize it as the same one.

The cast skin is known as exuviae, which might loosely be translated as "old clothes." The plural form of the word is always used in entomology. The throwing off of the old skin at periodic intervals is called molting, or ecdysis, and the periods between molts as stadia (singular, stadium). The form of an insect during a stadium is known as an instar. In describing the growth or development of an insect, both the stadia and instars are numbered. The first stadium is the period between hatching and the first molt, and the first instar is the form of the insect between hatching and the first molt. The second stadium is the period between the second and third molts, and the second instar the form during this period, and so on.

We shall now follow the growth of a young insect and observe the change of skin, or molting process. Almost any insect will serve, but the grasshopper is selected because it is a common and familiar insect and lends itself readily to certain observations. Also the eggs can be obtained throughout the winter, which is a good time to undertake a project of this sort. The eggs of the grasshopper may be obtained in two ways: by mating a pair of them and having the female lay the eggs in soil, or by buying the eggs.

If the grasshoppers are to be mated, we

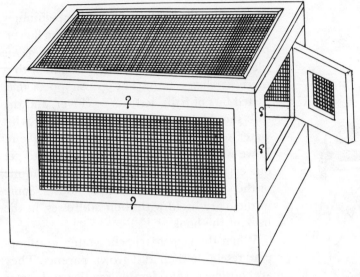

Figure 45
INSECT CAGE

shall have to get a male and female in late summer or early fall, when they become full-grown and before the cold kills them. For keeping the insects until they mate, an insect cage such as is shown in Figure 45 will serve. It can be made without too much effort and at little expense, but almost anything that can be converted into a terrarium will do. An aquarium tank such as is used for tropical fish, if filled with an inch or so of soil and covered at the top with a piece of screening so the grasshoppers cannot escape, will make an excellent terrarium. Perhaps the least expensive and certainly the easiest kind of ter-

Figure 46
REARING CHAMBER

rarium is the flowerpot-and-lamp-chimney arrangement shown in Figure 46. The flowerpot is filled with soil and the lamp chimney is placed firmly in the soil and covered with a piece of cheesecloth. The grasshoppers may be fed bits of fruit, lettuce, or clover, and the soil should be sprinkled occasionally with water to prevent the eggs from drying out. If we wait for sometime in the winter to get our eggs, we will have to buy them from one of the various biological supply houses. Some of them are listed with their addresses, in the back of the book.

When the eggs hatch, the young grasshoppers resemble their full-grown parents. They are, however, considerably smaller and somewhat differently proportioned (Figure 47). They cannot fly because they lack wings. Nor do they have any external reproductive appendages such as are present in the adults. Other than this the young and adults appear essentially alike.

To watch the young grasshoppers grow and change their skins at repeated intervals is highly interesting and informative, but our study can be made more definitive and scientific by making certain observations and recording them on a data sheet (Figure 48). Measure the size of the grasshoppers first when they emerge from the egg and again after the first molt, using a pair of calipers or dividers. Record the length in millimeters,

34

Figure 47
YOUNG GRASSHOPPER

obtained by placing the calipers or dividers against a metric scale. This is for the purpose of determining the amount of growth during the first stadium. The date of hatching and the date of molting should also be recorded to determine the time period of the first stadium. This same procedure is followed with

Figure 48
DATA SHEET

Data Sheet

Date	Number of Molt	Length	Period of Stadium	Amount of Growth	Daily Amount of Food	Amount of Food Eaten Each Stadium	Observations—Notes
	Hatching	mm	days	mm	grams	grams	

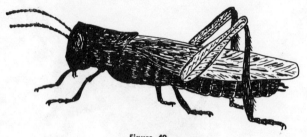

Figure 49
ADULT GRASSHOPPER

each successive stadium, and the amount of growth and the duration between molts recorded. The data sheet should also show various observations, as the stadium in which rudimentary wings appear and when the most striking change occurs, which will probably be during the last molt when the wings expand completely, the reproductive appendages appear, and the young grasshoppers become winged adults (Figure 49).

A record should also be kept of the amount of food eaten daily throughout their period of development. This is done by weighing the food given them each day (incidentally, fresh food should be given daily and any uneaten food removed) on a chemical or gram scale, which can be purchased from a biological supply house. The record of food quantities should include the amount given daily, the amount eaten during each stadium, and the total amount eaten from the time the eggs hatch to the final molt.

Young grasshoppers are known as nymphs. The word nymph is derived from the Greek word meaning "bride" or "maiden," and is applied not only to the young grasshoppers, but also to the immature forms of all insects in which there is a gradual growth of the body, wings, and reproductive appendages from the time the insects emerge from the egg until the last molt, when they become adults. Nymphs usually have no resting stage, as do the young of certain other insects like butterflies, beetles, flies, and bees. With·few exceptions their wings develop on the exterior of the body and they are generally terrestrial insects. They are also essentially plant feeders, although a few are predaceous, and in most cases both the nymphs and adults are injurious to crops or other vegetation.

CATERPILLARS ARE FAMILIAR to most of us. Every summer we find them in our gardens, along the roadside, in fields and woods, in. fact almost everywhere. Caterpillars eventually transform into butterflies and moths and represent the young or immature stage of these insects. Technically they are known as larvae (singular, larva). The word means "mask" in Latin and was originally applied to the caterpillars because the adult form was considered to be masked, or obscured, in the larva. The word is also applied to the young of such insects as the flies, beetles, wasps, bees, and ants, though the young of

ADVENTURE 5

*We Behold
a Miracle*

the flies are popularly known as maggots and those of the others as grubs.

In this adventure we are primarily interested in the caterpillars of butterflies. For our purpose the caterpillars of any species will do, and it doesn't matter how advanced they are in their growth, but it would be better to get the eggs, hatch them, and follow their development from the beginning, keeping a record of everything observed. Some of the easiest to find are the eggs of the milkweed butterfly since they are laid only on milkweed leaves and during the month of June, so this narrows our search. They are not difficult to recognize, for they are about the only eggs deposited on the milkweed. They are conical in shape, deeply ridged (Figure 50), and pale green in color. They are not removed from the leaf; instead the leaf is taken from the plant and placed in the flowerpot–lamp-chimney type of terrarium (Figure 46). That the leaf may remain fresh, the stem is inserted into a small bottle or vial of water which is sunk into the soil. To prevent the small caterpillars from falling into the water and drowning, cotton is stuffed into the neck of the bottle and covered with soil so the caterpillars will not become entangled in it.

Within a day or two after they have been laid, the eggs hatch into small, cylindrical caterpillars with alternate transverse bands of yellow, black, and white. The body is di-

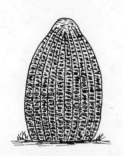

Figure 50
EGG OF MILKWEED BUTTERFLY

38

Figure 51

MILKWEED CATERPILLAR

vided into a number of segments, and there is a pair of threadlike, black "horns" on top of the second segment and a shorter pair on the eleventh (Figure 51). There are also three pairs of thoracic legs and several abdominal legs, or prolegs. The latter, which are armed with numerous minute hooks called crochets, help the caterpillars climb the plant.

As the caterpillars feed and move about, the black filaments or horns on the front part of the body move back and forth. If the caterpillars are disturbed or frightened, the horns twitch excitedly; those at the rear are quieter. These horns probably serve to keep away parasitic flies that lay their eggs upon the backs of the caterpillars if they get the chance. The caterpillars, like all caterpillars, have a voracious appetite and have to be given fresh food each day.

After several molts, when the caterpillar has reached its full growth, it spins a little silken mat on the milkweed leaf. In this silken mat it entangles the hooked claws of its feet. Then it lets go with its forefeet and hangs downward, with the front end of its body curled upward (Figure 52). It remains

Figure 52

SEMIPUPAL STAGE

39

Figure 53
SEMIPUPAL STAGE

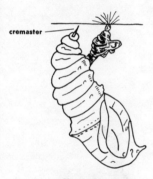

cremaster

Figure 54
SEMIPUPAL STAGE

Figure 55
CHRYSALIS OF MILKWEED BUTTERFLY

in this position for a few hours while the body juices gravitate downward and the lower segments assume a distended or swollen appearance. Suddenly the skin begins to split open along the median line of the back and gradually shrinks upward, being helped by the contortions of the caterpillar (Figure 53).

Meanwhile the caterpillar manages to engage a curious set of hooks, located on the posterior part of its body, in the silken mat (Figure 54). When these hooks are firmly in place, the skin drops off, exposing a strange-looking creature which is broader below than above. Soon the softer outer skin begins to harden into a distinct covering which assumes a beautiful green color, with a number of golden spots distributed over the surface and a few black spots just below the hooks (Figure 55). The insect now passes into a quiescent or resting period called the pupal stage and is itself known as a pupa.

During this period, which lasts about two weeks, some remarkable changes may be observed through the covering, which is thin and somewhat transparent. When the markings of the wings and the outline of the body may be seen quite clearly, the time for the butterfly to emerge is near. Now we can do one of two things: if we have the time, we can sit and wait for the butterfly to appear, or we can hasten its emergence by placing the pupa in the sunshine. Whichever we do, we sud-

40

denly observe the covering breaking apart over the head. At the same time the butterfly takes hold of the empty skin, as well as the support to which the skin is attached. It hangs downward, has a very large abdomen, and its wings are more or less crumpled up. The wings, however, soon begin to expand as the body juices enter the veins. The hind wings reach full size first, but soon both are fully expanded. Meanwhile the abdomen becomes smaller. At last the butterfly is able to walk a few steps and climb up the support, where it rests for an hour or so while its body and wing tissues harden. Then it is ready to take to wing and fulfill its mission in life, which is to mate and reproduce the species.

Figure 56
CHRYSALIS OF NORTHERN WOOD NYMPH

The pupa of a butterfly is called a chrysalis. The chrysalids of butterflies are not alike by any means. They vary greatly in shape and color. Some are plain, oval, and mummylike (Figure 56). Others have elaborately sculptured shapes or long spiny or knobby projections (Figure 57). Some are dull and plain, brown or green; others are brilliantly colored, sometimes with metallic gold or silver markings. In short they differ so markedly and are so distinctive of each species that we can identify a butterfly by its chrysalis alone.

In describing the change of the milkweed caterpillar to a pupa, we mentioned that the caterpillar attaches itself to the mat of silk by a curious set of hooks. Most butterfly pupae

Figure 57
CHRYSALIS OF MOURNING CLOAK

41

have a spiny process at the end of the posterior part of the body which may or may not be provided with hooks. This process is called a cremaster (Figure 54) and serves to hold the chrysalis after the larvel skin is shed. Some larvae also spin a girdle of silk to help keep the chrysalis in place (Figure 58).

ADVENTURE 6

We Find That Although a Leopard Cannot Change Its Spots, Other Animals Can

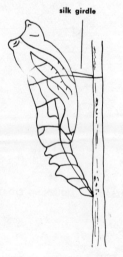

silk girdle

Figure 58
CHRYSALIS OF SWALLOWTAIL

EXCEPT FOR A gradual increase in size, the milkweed caterpillars, whose development we followed in the last adventure, remain unchanged in appearance. What happens 'in the case of certain other caterpillars, like those of the cecropia moth? Let us find eggs of this moth, hatch them, and find out. The eggs are laid on a variety of trees and shrubs, but since they are small and green in color are difficult to find. The best way to get them is to look for the cocoons in the wintertime, when they are conspicuous on the naked twigs and branches of the insect's food plant (Figure 59). The cocoons are removed from the twigs and placed in a container outdoors. A wooden box or any kind of container will do if the cocoons are exposed. It is best to leave the cocoons outdoors, where they can have the advantage of natural moisture and temperature. They can be left in a cool place indoors if necessary, but they should not be placed in a warm location, for if the caterpillars should appear before the leaves of the

42

Figure 59
COCOON OF CECROPIA MOTH

food plants have a chance to open, they will starve.

Once the leaves have begun to emerge from the buds in spring, the cocoons are transferred to an insect cage or terrarium large enough so the moths can fly about a little when they emerge from the cocoons. A few twigs should be placed in the terrarium for the moths to alight on. After the moths have emerged they mate, and the females lay their eggs on the leaves provided for them. We are not particularly limited to the kind of leaves and can use those of the apple, plum, cherry, grape, sassafras, or various species of willows, maples, ashes, and birches.

On emerging from the eggs, the caterpillars measure about a quarter of an inch long and are black in color, with each segment ornamented with six spiny tubercles, or warts. The first molt occurs about four days after the eggs are hatched. After casting the old skin, the caterpillars are dull orange or yel-

43

low with black tubercles. They feed for six or seven days and then molt again, emerging from the old skin with a yellow body. The two tubercles on top of each segment are now larger and more conspicuous. The tubercles on the first segment are blue, those on the second and third segment orange red, while those on the remaining segments, with the exception of the eleventh, are greenish blue with blackish spots and spines. Instead of a pair of tubercles on the eleventh segment, there is now one large tubercle ringed with black. The tubercles along the sides of the body are blue.

The next molt occurs five or six days later, and the caterpillars are now bluish green in color. The large tubercles on top of the second and third segments are deep orange or coral red, those of the first and last are blue, and all the others are yellow. The tubercles along the sides of the body are still blue. After the fourth molt the caterpillars are quite large (Figure 60), sometimes measuring as much as three inches. The colors remain essentially the same, although variation in the color of the tubercles may occur.

We have selected and followed the develop-

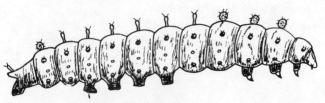

Figure 60
CATERPILLAR OF CECROPIA MOTH

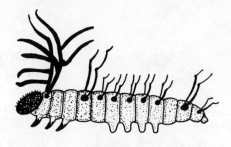

Figure 61
FIRST INSTAR LARVA
OF SADDLED PROMINENT

ment of the cecropia caterpillars simply to show that color changes may occur in successive molts. Should you undertake to study the development of any insect, especially those about which we know little, it is important to note and record such color changes. But color changes are not the only ones that may take place. A change in a particular structure or in the form of the body may also occur. The caterpillar of the saddled prominent, for instance, has in the first instar a pair of large antlerlike horns on the first thoracic segment and eight pairs of conspicuous horns on the abdominal segments (Figure 61). In the second instar all the horns are absent except small vestiges of the first pair (Figure 62). The larvae of certain leaf-mining insects are

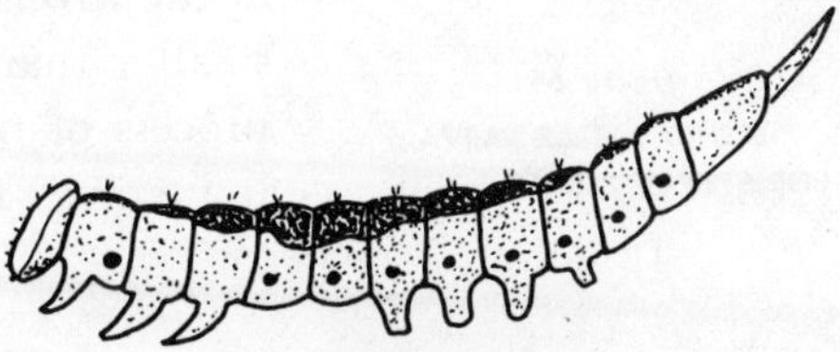

Figure 62
SECOND INSTAR LARVA
OF SADDLED PROMINENT

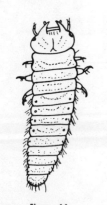

flat in the first, second, and third instars but cylindrical in the fourth and fifth. Even more remarkable are the changes that occur in the larva of the striped blister beetle. Figure 63 shows the larva during the first instar, Figure 64 during the second instar, Figure 65 during the third instar, and Figure 66 during the fifth instar.

There are many other interesting features associated with the process of molting. After each molt insects show a gain in appetite and their food consumption increases. It is often possible to determine the particular instar by the amount of food consumed. The size of the fecal pellets also increases with each successive molt. There is, however, a decrease in the period of the stadium—in other words, the rate of growth usually accelerates as the insect matures. The number of molts varies according to the species, but even in a given species the number may vary, depending on such conditions as moisture, temperature, and food supply. Experiments have shown that the clothes moth and carpet beetle, which feed on dry material, may continue to molt under starvation conditions, becoming smaller in size with each successive molt. It is well known that a deficient amount of food or the wrong kind of food will produce adults smaller than normal. Bear in mind that the process of molting is a delicate one because it involves not only the replacement of the external covering but also the lining of a considerable part of the digestive tract and respiratory system. The insect at this time is often inactive, helpless, and susceptible to injury. Many insects, therefore, seek a sheltered or secluded retreat like a folded leaf, in which to molt, while others spin a few silken threads to serve as a protective covering.

Figure 65
THIRD INSTAR LARVA
OF STRIPED BLISTER BEETLE

FOR OUR EXPERIMENTS we shall use meal worms, which can be obtained from any pet store at any time of the year. Meal worms have the distinction of being the only destructive insects purposely bred on a large scale for commercial purposes. They destroy vast quantities of flour, cereals, and various kinds of meal but are bred and sold as food for soft-billed birds and other pets like lizards, salamanders, and fish.

Meal worms are the larvae of two beetles known scientifically as *Tenebrio obscurus* and *Tenebrio molitor*. The larvae of both are hard and cylindrical (Figure 67); *obscurus* is yellow in color, shading off somewhat into yellowish brown at each end, whereas *molitor* is a little lighter. The pupae are whitish and about half an inch long, with most of the abdominal segments fringed with side expansions and the last one furnished with two spines (Figure 68). The adults of both species are black or dark reddish brown (Figure 69)

ADVENTURE 7

We Undertake Some Experiments with Feeding Insects

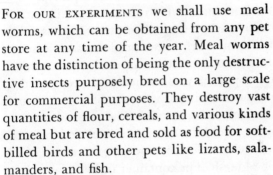

Figure 66
FIFTH INSTAR LARVA
OF STRIPED BLISTER BEETLE

Figure 67
LARVA OF *TENEBRIO*

47

Figure 68
PUPA OF TENEBRIO

Figure 69
ADULT OF TENEBRIO

and about half an inch long. The only apparent difference between the two is that *molitor* is shiny.

Before any experiments can be conducted, it will be necessary to obtain the eggs. As the eggs cannot be bought in a pet store, the meal worms are raised into adults that will mate and provide the eggs. It will not be necessary to buy many, probably a dozen or so. For raising the meal worms, either a pint jar or a small wooden box from four to six inches deep may be used. The jar or box is filled with fine corn meal or flour and a small amount of bran to within an inch or so from the top. Fine whole wheat or a prepared dog meal containing dried vegetables, cereals, and meat may also be used. The meal worms are next placed in the jar or box and covered with cheesecloth or fine wire screening of 20 or 24 mesh. The container is then placed in a location where the temperature will remain at about 25° C and at a relative humidity of 75-80 per cent. (This means that a centigrade thermometer and a hygrometer must be procured. The thermometer isn't expensive but the hygrometer will run into a little money, so if you cannot buy either or both, perhaps you can borrow these instruments from your school or perhaps your teacher will permit you to rear meal worms in the science laboratory.) Once the meal worms have hatched, they require no further attention until the late larval instars, when the food should be changed at least once a month.

When the larvae are ready to pupate, they come to the top of the meal and pass into a quiescent state. They are now kept under observation, and when the adults appear they are placed in an ovipositing cage. For such a cage a pint-sized cardboard container with the bottom pushed out and replaced with a 20- mesh wire screening is used. The mesh will allow the eggs to fall through readily. The top is covered with a piece of screening and the cover of the container is placed beneath the ovipositing cage for collecting the eggs. In the cover a little whole-wheat flour sifted through a 72- mesh silk screen is placed, and in the ovipositing cage a few dog biscuits as food for the adults. To stimulate oviposition, a small wire basket containing moist food such as a piece of meat or banana is suspended from the top of the cage. When the adults have mated and the females have oviposited, the eggs are collected by sifting the flour through a 30- mesh silk screen.

After the eggs have been collected, we can try feeding the hatched meal worms various kinds of meals and other foods which we think will prove suitable. Round, pint-sized containers, filled separately with a different kind of food and in each of which a few eggs are placed, may be used. Then all the containers are placed in the same location, where all will be subjected to the same conditions of temperature and humidity. Or a number of containers may be filled with the same kind of food and each one placed in a different location, where each will be subjected to different temperatures and humidity—as, for instance, a cellar, an attic, garage, etc. Of course for more scientific results they should be placed in a temperature-controlled incubator such as is used for hatching chickens. Such an incubator is readily made of a wooden box with glass sides and top and with an electric light bulb to provide heat. With such an incubator constant temperature and humidity can be maintained. With the food mentioned above and an environment maintained at 30°C and 80 per cent relative humidity, *molitor* may be reared from egg to adult stage in less than four months. Perhaps you can accelerate the growth of meal worms and reduce this time period. One more thing —as far as I know, the optimum food for meal worms is not yet definitely known.

Those of you who are scientifically-minded can improvise and experiment in countless ways. Bear in mind that no experiment is of value unless a complete record is kept of everything you do and the results obtained. Once you have experimented with meal worms, there is an unlimited number of other insects to serve as subjects for experimentation.

GO DOWN TO THE BANK of a fresh-water stream, pond, or lake and watch the dragonflies speed through the air, darting here and there after some luckless victim. You will be fascinated by their aerial maneuvers. In the adjoining field or meadow you will likely see a butterfly or two flying lazily about, taking an apparently aimless and erratic course. Perhaps a bee or wasp will fly swiftly by. You may see a beetle, frightened or disturbed, take to the air and then quickly alight on a bush. Even a grasshopper may leap up from the ground and disappear in the distance. Compare the flight habits of these and other insects and you will find they show marked differences.

You may think that the larger the wings, the better an insect is able to fly, but after a moment's comparison of the butterfly with the dragonfly you will quickly dismiss such an idea. Size has little to do with it; the dobson fly has two large wings but is a clumsy flier. The golden eye also has comparatively large wings but is a poor flier. And certainly a butterfly cannot match the speed or the aerial gymnastics of a dragonfly. Some of the larger dragonflies have been clocked at sixty miles an hour—but this speed, fast as it is, is nothing compared to the speed of the male botfly, which has been estimated at eight hundred and eighteen miles an hour. Moths, with their relatively large wings, are in the same class as butterflies and are not particularly capable fliers except for the sphingid moth, whose wings are narrow and not widely expanded, as are the wings of moths in general. Nor indeed does the number of wings determine an insect's ability to fly. The housefly has only one pair, but try to catch one! Indeed it seems as if the true flies, with a single pair of wings, are better off than the other insects when it comes to flying.

It is well known that man learned to fly by studying the flight of birds and insects. The dynamics of flight and the design of aircraft have to do with air lift, drag, and differences in air velocity. The mechanism of insect flight appears similarly complex, but it is actually less so because, owing to the structure of the wing itself, up-and-down movements are sufficient for the simplest kind of flight. During oscillation—that is, up-and-down movement —the plane of the wing changes. You can demonstrate this by removing a wing (after first killing the insect), holding it by its base, and then blowing at right angles to its surface. The membrane of the wing yields to the pressure of the air while the rigid anterior margin does not, to any great extent. In a similar manner, as the wings move downward the membrane is inclined upward by the resistance of the air, and as the wing moves upward the membrane bends downward. By becoming deflected, the wing meets a certain amount of air resistance from behind, which is enough to propel the insect. The faster the wings vibrate, the greater the deflection, the greater the resistance from behind, and the faster the flight.

The path traced in the air by a rapidly vibrating wing may be shown by attaching a bit of gold leaf to the tip of a wing and then allowing the insect to vibrate its wings in the sunlight against a dark background. Carry out this experiment and you will find that the trajectory of the wing appears as a luminous, elongated figure 8. Or hold the insect in the beam of light of a film projector so that the insect is projected on a screen. In flight the trajectory consists of a continuous series of these figures (Figure 70).

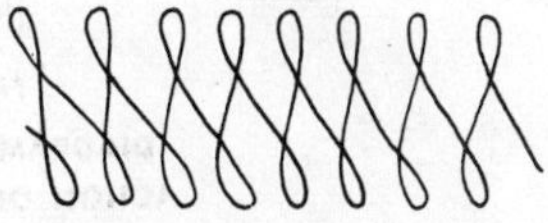

The frequency of wing vibration—that is, the number of vibrations in a given period of time—may be determined from the note made by the wing, provided the wing vibrates rapidly enough to make one. Simply hold an insect like a housefly, for instance, in such a position that each stroke of the wing makes a record on a piece of smoked paper or glass as shown in Figure 71. Then compare this record with those made by tuning forks of known frequencies.

The smaller the wings the greater the frequency, or the more rapidly they vibrate. A butterfly makes nine strokes per second, a dragonfly thirty, a sphingid moth seventy-two, a bee one hundred and ninety, and a

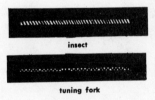

Figure 70
TRAJECTORY OF THE WING OF AN INSECT

insect

tuning fork

Figure 71
RECORD OF WING VIBRATION

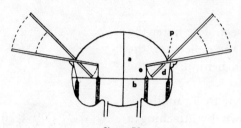

housefly three hundred and thirty.

To be able to move its wings an insect has to have muscles, and the stronger the flight, the more powerful the muscles. By referring to Figure 72, you can get some idea of how the muscles operate the wing. The base of the wing projects into the thoracic cavity and serves for the insertion of the direct muscles in flight. Regard the wing as a lever with the fulcrum at p and you can easily understand how the contraction of muscle e raises the wing and that of muscle d lowers it. In addition to these muscles there are others that act indirectly upon the wings by altering the form of the thoracic wall. Thus the muscle a elevates the wing by drawing the top of the thorax toward the bottom and the muscle b depresses the wing by pulling the sides of the thorax together and arching the top of the thorax. This explains the simplest kind of insect flight, but in insects that are efficient and powerful fliers, like the dragonflies, the process is somewhat more complicated, as

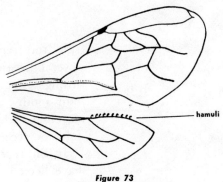

Figure 73
WINGS OF THE HONEYBEE

more muscles are involved. Thus in the drag-onflies there are nine muscles to each wing: five depressors, three elevators, and one ad-ductor.

Much as the oarsmen of a boat can obtain greater efficiency with their oars if they all pull together, an insect can make greater use of its wings if the fore and hind wings act in unison. The synchronous action of the two wings is obtained in some insects by the fore wing overlapping the hind wing, but in other species certain structures have been developed which fasten together the two wings of each side. Obtain a honeybee and examine the outer costal margin of the hind wing and you will find a row of hooks, called hamuli, which fasten into a fold on the inner margin of the forewing (Figure 73). Next examine the hind wing of a moth, where you will find at the humeral angle a strong, spinelike organ or bunch of bristles called the frenulum, or little bridle (Figure 74). As a

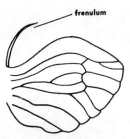

Figure 74
HIND WING
OF THE BAGWORM MOTH

55

rule, the frenulum of the female consists of several bristles; in the male it is a single, strong, spinelike organ. In the males of certain moths where the frenulum is highly developed, the fore wing has a membranous fold for receiving the end of the frenulum.

In the true flies the second pair of wings have been replaced by knobbed, threadlike organs called halteres. These organs are also known as balancers, because at one time it was believed they functioned in the same manner as the weighed pole carried by tight-rope walkers. Recent investigations, however, have shown that they act in a different manner.

Actually they vibrate very rapidly during flight. Their frequency is about the same as the wing beat, but they are usually in anti-phase with the wings. A single muscle causes the upbeat of the halteres and there is no antagonistic muscle, the downbeat being brought about by the elastic nature of the hinge. Furthermore the two halteres do not move in the same plane, as each is angled posteriorly.

If you understand the mechanics of a gyro-scope, you will have some idea of how the halteres function, for they work precisely like a gyroscope. We might simply say that in insect flight the halteres are the counterpart of a bank-and-turn indicator.

WE OFTEN WONDER how the mosquito punctures our skin and sucks our blood and why the act should lead too such intense itching. The structures with which the mosquito is provided for her bloodsucking act (only the female can do this) are rather complicated and, the better to understand them, it is best to examine first the mouth parts of some other sucking insect, one that sucks nectar, like a butterfly.

On a bright sunny day in summer visit some flowers frequented by butterflies and wait patiently for one to appear. A reading glass will be helpful, although you can see the butterfly feeding with your naked eye. The moment a butterfly alights on a flower, watch closely and observe that it uncurls a long, tonguelike organ and extends it into the flower. This tonguelike organ, called a proboscis, is normally kept coiled beneath the head (Figure 75), and when the insect is feeding it is unwound like a watch spring. To learn how the proboscis is put together capture a butterfly and, after killing it, ex-

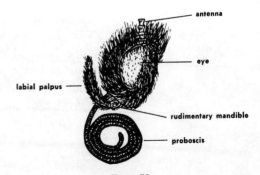

Figure 75
HEAD OF A BUTTERFLY

amine the proboscis with a hand lens or microscope. It is composed of the two maxillae, which fit together to form a tube. The maxillae, as you recall, are the lower jaws. Also note that the labrum is reduced and the mandibles, which are of no value for sucking purposes, are either rudimentary or absent. The labium is also reduced, though the labial palpi are much in evidence. How is the nectar drawn up the tube? Dissect the head with a razor blade and locate a bulb which is dilated and compressed alternately by numerous muscles. Much like the action of a medicine dropper, this produces a partial vacuum and results in the nectar's being drawn up the tube and passed back into the stomach. This description applies equally to the moths, but in both the butterflies and moths there occur minor variations. In some species there are well-developed maxillary palpi, and in others the tips of the maxillae are provided with spines which enable the insects to lacerate the tissues of ripe fruits, thus setting juices free to be sucked up. In still other species that do not feed at all, the maxillae are entirely wanting.

Next look for some feeding squash bugs (Figure 76) and observe through your lens that instead of a proboscis, a beaklike organ extends downward from the head and into the surface of the leaf. Examine this organ more closely and you will find it is actually

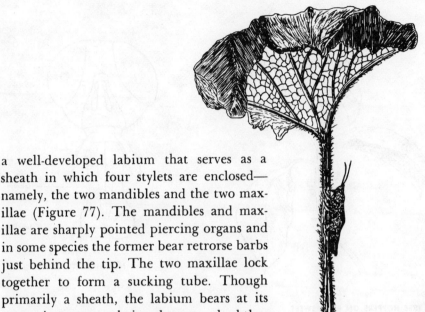

a well-developed labium that serves as a
sheath in which four stylets are enclosed—
namely, the two mandibles and the two maxillae (Figure 77). The mandibles and maxillae are sharply pointed piercing organs and
in some species the former bear retrorse barbs
just behind the tip. The two maxillae lock
together to form a sucking tube. Though
primarily a sheath, the labium bears at its
extremity sensory hairs that are doubtless
used to test the food. The labrum is usually
short and inconspicuous. A pumping or suc-
tion apparatus similar to that found in butterflies and moths is also present.

Figure 76
SQUASH BUG

As you observe various species of sucking
insects feeding, you will note that they exhibit a diversity of habits. Some of them
puncture leaves; others, stems; and still
others, fruits. Many of them assume characteristic attitudes when feeding. If you can
locate a bittersweet vine you may find a
group of tree hoppers on it. Look carefully
and you will see that no matter how much
the vine twists and turns, the little hoppers

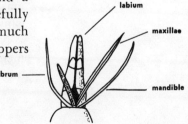

labium

maxillae

labrum

mandible

Figure 77

Figure 78
TREE HOPPERS ON BITTERSWEET

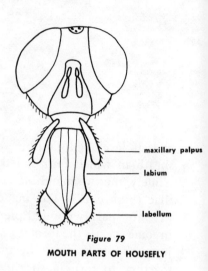

maxillary palpus

labium

labellum

Figure 79
MOUTH PARTS OF HOUSEFLY

all sit with their heads toward the top so the sap will flow more easily down their throats (Figure 78).

Just as the feeding habits of true flies vary considerably, the mouth parts show various modifications. In some species they are developed for piercing and sucking; in others, for lapping and sucking. They consist, in the more typical forms, of six bristlelike organs enclosed in a sheath and a pair of jointed palpi. In the housefly the labium and the maxillary palpi are the most conspicous organs (Figure 79).

Now we come to the mosquito, also a member of the group of flies. This pestiferous and sometimes dangerous insect is usu-

60

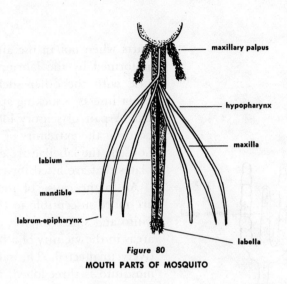

maxillary palpus

hypopharynx

maxilla

labium

mandible

labrum-epipharynx

labella

Figure 80

MOUTH PARTS OF MOSQUITO

ally available throughout the summer, and
if we allow the female to "bite" we can,
through our lens, watch her suck our blood.
To examine her mouth parts we need a microscope, as they are extremely small. We
capture and kill one, place it on a microscope
slide, and transfer the slide to the stage of
the microscope. We adjust the low objective
until the mouth parts come into focus. At this
point we may have to separate the mouth
parts with a needle. They are long and slender. The mandibles and maxillae are delicate,
linear piercing organs, the latter barbed
distally, and it is with these that the insect
punctures our skin (Figure 80). The labium
forms a sheath enclosing the other mouth

61

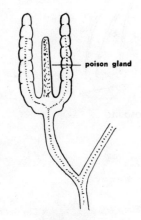

poison gland

Figure 81
SALIVARY GLANDS OF MOSQUITO

parts when not in use and the sucking tube is formed by the labrum, which is not the case with the other sucking insects. As in other insects, a sucking apparatus is also present. A pair of sensory lobes, termed labella, occur at the extremity of the labium. (In the housefly the labellae are extended into broad plates that are fitted for rasping.)

As to the cause of itching. Some people are more susceptible to the "bite" of a mosquito and suffer intense itching and swollen areas in the vicinity of a bite; others are relatively unaffected. The salivary gland of the mosquito is three-lobed, as shown in Figure 81, and it will be seen that the middle lobe differs in appearance from the other two. This middle lobe secretes a poisonous fluid that is carried out along the tongue when the female punctures the skin and is injected into the wound. The purpose of this fluid is probably to prevent the blood from coagulating. At any rate, it is this fluid that causes the itching.

Although most people regard mosquitoes as bloodsucking insects, there are many species that do not suck blood at all, and of those that do, only the females are able to do so. The mouth parts of the males are not suited for puncturing the skins of animals; hence they feed on nectar, the juices of fruits, and other sweet substances. Even the females that suck blood may feed on these substances.

ALL INSECTS DEPEND on plants, either directly or indirectly (predators and parasites feed on plant-eating forms) for their existence. Plant-eating insects feed on all parts of the plant— bud, flower, leaf, stem, root, fruit, seed—and its secretions—sap, nectar, and other juices. No part of a plant is immune. Nor do many plants escape the ravages of some insect pest. The ginkgo and ailanthus may be the exceptions, as they have few or no insect enemies. Even the poison ivy, which we would expect to be avoided, is host to several species.

For the most part plants are helpless against insect depredations, although some plants have devised various means for repelling them. These devices take the form of hairs, spines, acrid juices, and extreme toughness of tissues, but they are only partially effective. Other plants like the pitcher plant, sundew, and Venus flytrap have developed structures for capturing or entrapping insects that venture too near. Certain bacteria infect them with disease, like the flacherie of the silkworm and the milky disease of the Japanese beetle, and certain fungi penetrate and destroy them with their fungal threads.

It is not in these one-sided relationships or associations that we are interested, but those where both the plants and insects are of benefit to one another. These associations are founded essentially on an exchange of pollen and nectar; in other words the insects

We Find Out How Plants and Insects Help One Another

63

visit the flowers to obtain their nectar and in return pollinate the flowers. Cross-fertilization is a necessity for the continued vigor and fertility of flowering plants, and while some plants depend on the wind to accomplish this, most of them rely on the insects.

Such dependency might seem to be an uncertain means of ensuring the survival of a plant species, and it probably would be if the plants depended entirely on accidental visits. That such visits might not be left completely to chance, the plants seek to attract the insects by conspicuous colors and distinctive odors. Night-blooming flowers, for instance, are often white or yellow and, as a rule, strongly scented so they can be located by nocturnal insects. Colors and odors, however, simply serve notice to the insects that nectar and pollen are available and do not guarantee that they will respond. At least that is what we believe, and it is probably true that insects actually do associate color and nectar, even though they will fly to bits of colored paper as readily as they will fly to flowers of the same color. That the insects realize they confer any benefit upon the plant whose flowers they visit for food is unlikely; it is an entirely unconscious act on their part.

We must also bear in mind that not every insect that visits a flower for nectar returns the favor. Some of them are pilferers, stealing the nectar without giving anything in

64

return. Bumblebees, for instance, puncture the nectaries of such plants as snapdragons and columbine and surreptitiously sip the nectar. Certain wasps cut through the corolla, making a hole opposite each nectary, and take the floral juices without so much as a thank you. A few moths are able to extend their proboscises between the petals and suck the nectar without even entering the flower.

In many instances the process of insect pollination is a simple one; the insect brushes against the anthers of a flower and becomes dusted with pollen, which it carries to the next flower. Many plants, however, have become so modified that only certain insects can enter the flowers to obtain the nectar, and they cannot do so without leaving some pollen or carrying some away. Consider the common blue flag or iris, a flower remarkably adapted for such an interchange.

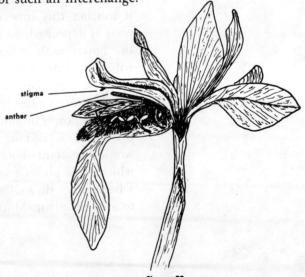

stigma

anther

Figure 82
BEE VISITING IRIS

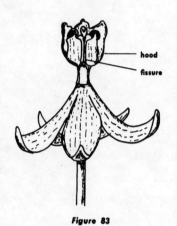

Figure 83
FLOWER OF MILKWEED

hood

fissure

Examine the flower carefully and you will find that each of the three drooping sepals forms the floor of an arched passageway leading to the nectar that is located in deep pockets (Figure 82). Note further that over the entrance and pointing outward is a movable lip. This lip is the stigma. When an insect such as a bee enters the passageway, it brushes against the sticky surface of the stigma and bends it down. Then as the bee pushes its head farther into the passageway to collect the nectar, the lip or stigma scrapes from the insect's back pollen collected from a flower previously visited. Meanwhile the hairy back of the bee rubs against an overhanging anther and becomes powdered with grains of pollen. Once the bee has obtained its fill of nectar, it backs out of the passageway and, as it does so, again encounters the guardian lip—but as the side of the lip which it touches this time cannot receive pollen, none is deposited. So the bee is able to leave the flower with a load of pollen, which it will in turn deposit on the stigma of the next flower it visits. You may ask whether it is not possible for the bee to enter another part of the same flower or another flower of the same plant and deposit its load of pollen, which would be tantamount to self-pollination, which most plants avoid. There is no reason a bee cannot do so, but insects habitually fly to another plant. Moreover foreign pollen is

66

prepotent over pollen from the same flower, so that self-pollination is unlikely.

The common milkweed is another familiar plant ingeniously constructed to ensure pollination by insects. It has special pollen masses, called pollinia, that are so arranged that when an insect steps upon the edge of the flower to sip nectar, its legs slip between the peculiar nectariferous hoods situated in front of each anther (Figure 83). As the insect then draws its legs upward, a claw, hair, or spine frequently catches in a V-shaped fissure and is guided along a slit to a notched disk which becomes attached to the leg. Since the pollen masses or pollinia are each connected to the disk by a stalk, they are carried off when the insect leaves (Figure 84). Upon the insect's arrival at another milkweed flower, the pollinia are easily introduced into the stigmatic chamber. The struggles of the insect at this time break the stalks of the pollinia, and the insect is relieved of its load. Sometimes the insect loses a leg in its struggle or is permanently entrapped.

You can observe the details of insect pollination in both the iris and milkweed by watching the behavior of an insect through a magnifying glass when it alights on the flowers. Or you can demonstrate the process of pollination in the milkweed by capturing an insect just as it leaves the flower with the pollinia dangling from its legs. Kill it, re-

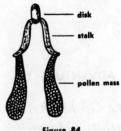

Figure 84
POLLINIA OF MILKWEED

67

move one of its legs, and then draw the leg upward between the two hoods of the flower to remove first the pair of pollinia and then to introduce one of them into an empty stigmatic chamber.

ADVENTURE 11

We Go Marketing with the Honeybee and Other Insects

Figure 85
POLLEN-GATHERING HAIR OF WORKER HONEYBEE

INSECTS LIKE THE bumblebee and honeybee, which collect pollen that they convert into beebread, a form of food suitable for their young, must obviously be provided with some means of carrying the pollen. The insects that visit flowers for nectar and pollen may be variously modified to be more effective as agents of pollination. The adaptations are not as manifold nor as exquisite as those of the plants, since the plants had to adjust themselves to the insects as a matter of vital necessity, yet the insects have to some extent been influenced by floral structure and many of them have been uniquely modified structurally and physiologically to accommodate them to the flowers they visit.

Many pollen-gathering insects—that is, insects that feed on pollen—are provided with hairs that are usually dense and often twisted, branched, or barbed. Examine the pollen-gathering hair of a worker bee and you will find it looks as shown in Figure 85. Some insects like the mining bees, the bee flies, flower flies, and the pollen-feeding flower beetles have mouth parts densely clothed

68

with hairs (Figure 86). A few bees are provided with pollen baskets, or corbicula. In the honeybee these pollen baskets áre on the outer surface of each hind tibia.

To examine one of these pollen baskets with a hand lens, we must capture a bee and then subject it to the fumes of the killing jar. A killing jar is a bottle or jar with a screw top and a piece of cotton attached to the lower surface of the cover so the cotton will hang downward. The cotton is soaked in a fluid that will kill the insect and evaporate quickly. Carbon tetrachloride, which can be purchased at a drug store, will do. It is not inflammable but it is best not to inhale too much of it. When the insect shows no signs of life, we remove it and look at the hind legs. We should, if the bee has been on a collecting trip, find attached to each one a roundish, yellowish, sticky mass. This is pollen dust, the flour which it would have used to make the beebread. We remove the pollen from one of the legs with a small brush and then look at the tibia with our lens. We shall find it is fashioned into a sort of receptacle (Figure 87) which is the basket, or corbiculum.

To see how the bee fills its baskets, station yourself near a flower visited by honeybees and with a reading glass watch the bee as it climbs over the flower. Look closely and you will see that the flexible, branching hairs with which the body and legs are covered

Figure 86
MANDIBLE OF POLLEN-FEEDING FLOWER BEETLE

pollen basket

Figure 87
HIND LEG OF WORKER HONEYBEE

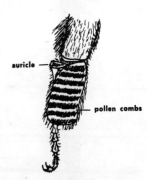

auricle

pollen combs

Figure 88
INNER SURFACE OF HIND LEG

69

Figure 89
AURICLE OF HIND LEG

— spur

Figure 90
PART OF MIDDLE LEG

— labellum

Figure 91
TONGUE OF HONEYBEE

entangle the pollen grains. With special structures called pollen combs, located on the inner surface of the hind tarsus (Figure 88), the bee combs the pollen grains out of the hairs and transfers them to the baskets, at the same time, to fill them to capacity, pressing the pollen down into the baskets by means of the auricle (Figure 89). On the bee's return to the hive it thrusts its hind legs into a cell and then, with a spur located at the apex of the middle tibia (Figure 90), pries off the pollen, the spur being slipped in at the upper end of the corbiculum and then pushed along the tibia under the mass of pollen.

In addition to these structures for gathering pollen the honeybee has an exceptionally long tongue, compared with that of other bees, enabling the insect to reach deep into the flowers. Furthermore the tongue is also beautifully specialized for lapping up and sucking nectar, as shown in Figure 91. Most insect pollinators, as a matter of fact, have unusually long tongues. This is particularly true of the sphinx moths, in which the length of the tongue bears a direct relation to the depth of the nectaries of the flowers they visit.

70

CONSIDERING THE THINNESS of a leaf, it doesn't seem possible there are insects so small that they can live and grow between the upper and lower surfaces. You have doubtless seen leaves discolored and disfigured by blotches (Figure 92) and winding lines (Figure 93) and perhaps did not know they were made by insects.

Insects that live between the two epidermal surfaces of a leaf are known as leaf miners. As a rule they are flat without legs and setae, or bristles, but if these structures are present they are much reduced (Figure 94). The head is often wedge-shaped, thus being an efficient device for separating the two epidermal layers as the insect moves forward, and is also sometimes rotated to a horizontal position and telescoped into the thorax. In some species the antennae and eyes are reduced and in others the eyes are arranged alongside the head. The jaws are usually sharp and operated by powerful muscles. In the sap-feeding species the mandibles are platelike with many sharp teeth for cutting through plant cells to make the sap flow. Hard plates, or tubercles, are sometimes present to help the insect maintain a firm hold as it feeds within the mine or tunnel it excavates.

Leaf miners are essentially immature insects and remain within the leaf only until they have become fully grown, when they

71

We Encounter a Problem in Waste Disposal

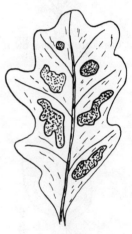

Figure 92
BLOTCH MINES ON OAK

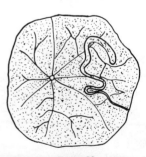

Figure 93
LINEAR MINE ON NASTURTIUM

Figure 94
LINEAR-BLOTCH MINE ON ELM

Figure 95
TRUMPET MINES ON APPLE

Figure 96
DIGITATE MINE ON LOCUST

transform into winged adults. If you hold a green leaf discolored by a blotch or a winding line up to a light, you can watch the insect feed. You will note that a winding or linear mine increases in width with length (Figure 93); this is necessary to accommodate an increase in size on the part of the insect. The blotch and linear mines frequently assume different shapes and often intergrade with one another.

There are two general types of mines: linear (Figure 93) and blotch (Figure 92). Modifications of both occur, as the linear-blotch (Figure 94), trumpet (Figure 95), digitate (Figure 96), and tentiform. If the insect first makes a linear mine and then suddenly expands it into a blotch, the result is a linear-blotch mine. If the insect gradually broadens its passageway, a trumpet mine is formed. And if the insect spins silk within the mine, the mine is thrown into a fold when the silk shrinks and becomes tentiform in shape. Linear mines may be straight, curved, or winding. A winding mine is called a serpentine mine, since it is shaped like a serpent (Figure 93). Blotch mines are broad patches of almost any size and shape, and increase in size as the miners feed and grow.

The feeding habits of the leaf miners determine to a large extent the location of the mine. Some species feed only on the palisade layer; (Figure 97) their mines are therefore

72

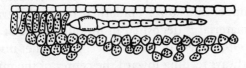

Figure 97

LEAF MINE IN PALISADE LAYER

made only on the upper surface of the leaf
and are visible only from the upper side.
Miners that feed on the parenchyma cells excavate tunnels in the lower surface, and their
mines are visible only from the lower side.
Species that feed on both kinds of cells form
tunnels that are visible from both sides. Some
mines are made near the center of the leaf,
others along the edge.

If we make a study of the leaf miners, we
find that their feeding habits vary. The
polygon leaf miner, so called because its
mines are small and often rectangular, feeds
from the outside toward the middle of the
mine; hence it must first mark the final area
to be mined before it begins feeding, otherwise its food supply would be exhausted
before it matured. During the first two instars
it is a sap feeder, working on the lower surface of the mine and feeding upon the liquid
contents of the cell. After the third molt the
insect becomes a tissue feeder but does not
extend the range of its mine; instead it goes

back over the rectangular area previously covered and strips all the cells between the upper and lower epidermal layers. All waste material is deposited in minute pellets at the outer edge of the mine. Thus the insect, always feeding toward the center of the mine, has a continual supply of fresh food uncontaminated by fecal matter.

Unlike the polygon leaf miner, most miners feed entirely on the sap or the tissues. Linear miners usually feed upon the cell sap, blotch miners on the tissues, either on the palisade layer or on the parenchyma cells. Frequently an entire family feeds together, making a large and ugly blotch mine. If we hold up to the light a mined leaf of dock or beet while it is still green, we can see several insects working, each making a bag in the tissues of the leaf and all joining together to make a great blister. Some species have developed the habit of entering new leaves when their food supply has become exhausted or when the leaves wilt or otherwise become undesirable.

As mines serve as a shelter, albeit a temporary one, they provide a measure of protection for the developing insects. The insects, however, are not entirely safe from their enemies, as various predaceous and parasitic forms manage to gain access to them. Aside from this, it would seem that their larval existence would be an enviable one, living as they do in a world of abundance with nothing to think about except to eat and grow. But all is not quite that rosy. They have two major problems. One is not to cut the latex cells, lest the sap flow out and drown them. The.other is how to get rid of waste material, or frass.

The first is easily solved by being careful not to cut the cells. The second problem has several solutions. The primitive miners have solved it by spreading the frass in an even layer on the lower surface of the mine. These miners make blotch or blotchlike mines and, as a rule, feed along the outer edge, where the food remains uncontaminated. A miner that excavates in the leaves of the hop horn-beam illustrates this habit. The insect feeds only on the palisade layer and makes an ex-ceedingly shallow mine which may cover the entire area of the leaf. Indeed, the mine is so shallow that when completed, the parchment-like upper surface can be removed like a sheet of paper. If you can find one of these mined leaves, you will find that the frass is smeared over the entire floor of the mine and appears as black masses (Figure 98).

A small fly that mines in the leaves of the Cruciferae excavates a digitate mine and has found the fingerlike projections suitable dis-posal chambers. Another miner, which tun-nels in the upper surface of locust leaves, excavates a small subcuticular mine on the

Figure 98
BLOTCH MINE SHOWING FRASS DISPOSAL

75

Figure 99
LINEAR MINE SHOWING
FRASS DISPOSAL

Figure 100
BLOTCH MINE SHOWING
FRASS DISPOSAL

lower surface into which it pushes its fecula. A third species, which lives in basswood leaves, has solved the problem of frass disposal by feeding toward the center and leaving its excrement at the outer edge of the mine. Another species reverses the process.

Some of the linear miners have found a rather simple solution: they merely leave their wastes behind as they eat their way forward. In some of these species the frass is laid down in a single continuous central line (Figure 99); in others, in an interrupted central line; and in still others, two parallel lines are formed, one on each side of the mine. Certain miners, like the apple leaf miner, are more fastidious. They make small holes in the surface of the leaf and push their fecula out through them (Figure 100). The frass emerges in small pellets that adhere to one another like minute links of a sausage.

Mines are conspicuous on the leaves of many plants from the middle of summer to autumn. The type of mine and the plant on which it is made are usually characteristic of the species that made it and often serve as a clue to its maker. Mines are easily collected and preserved by removing the entire leaves and pressing them between newspapers or a pulp magazine until dry. By making a collection of mined leaves and referring to books on insects, you can become acquainted with the various species of leaf miners. Moreover,

76

since a mine often reveals the complete life history of the insect, the mines lend themselves readily to worth-while ecological studies. It is possible to determine from a mine the position of the egg, the type of feeding, and the number of molts, while the cast larval and pupal skins often remain to complete the story. If you are interested in such a study, mark a mined leaf by tying a string loosely around the stalk and then keep a record of all you observe. Drawings will help. If the insect pupates in the leaf, remove the leaf, place it in a jar covered with a piece of thin cloth, and leave the jar in a sheltered spot outdoors until the adult emerges. If the miners leave their mines and pupate elsewhere, you might try to locate the pupating insects and if you find them, place them in a covered jar as described.

IF WE PAUSE by the edge of a pond or stream or even by a large puddle around the beginning of summer, we are likely to see a slender black or brown wasp with yellow spots and yellow legs running up and down and digging here and there in the mud. Suddenly we see it plunge its head into the mud and, seeming to stand on its head, wave its abdomen about in the air.

The wasp is a mason, or cement worker, and is seeking the right kind of mud with

ADVENTURE 13

We Watch Some Masons at Work

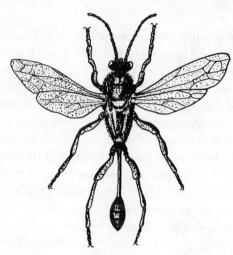

which to build a nest or home for her young.

Most of us have seen what appears to be a daub of mud stuck against the side of a building or on the rafter of a barn or upon the wall or beam of an unfinished attic. Actually the daub of mud is a well-contrived nest and is built by a wasp called the mud dauber (Figure 101)—a rather uncomplimentary term, for the nest is cleverly and skillfully constructed despite its somewhat slovenly external appearance (Figure 102).

In building her nest, the wasp first selects a suitable place—say, a rafter—and then goes searching for her mud. She cuts a small pellet about the size of a sweet-pea seed, which she mixes with her own saliva. When it is

Figure 102
NEST OF MUD DAUBER

prepared to the proper consistency, she attaches the pellet to the rafter and returns to her source for another. She repeats the performance until she has built a foundation of mud. She gradually fashions a tube about an inch long with walls about one eighth of an inch thick. At the same time she smooths the inside walls, but is unconcerned about the exterior and leaves it rough. She does all this work with her jaws, using them as a sort of trowel.

Eventually she completes the tube to her satisfaction and at this point drops her role of mason and becomes a hunter, going off in search of a spider. When she finds one she stings it, perhaps repeatedly or until she has immobilized but not killed it, for this would defeat her purpose, and carries it to her tube and thrusts it inside. Again she goes in search of a spider, which she stings and adds to the first one. She continues her search for spiders until she has filled the tube with them. Then she lays an egg in the tube and closes it with more mud. With the egg safely tucked away, sufficient food stored for the young to feed on when it hatches, and its little home securely closed, the wasp builds another tube next to the original one, which she provisions and closes after having laid an egg in it. She may build several more tubes or she may be satisfied with two, but when she has finished building her full complement of tubes or

Figure 103
TWO CELLS OF MUD DAUBER
(Left: COCOON, Right: LARVA)

Figure 104
NESTS OF PIPE-ORGAN DAUBER

cells, she smears them all over with a coating of mud. When the young larva emerges from the egg, it feeds on the spiders and when full-grown, spins a silken cocoon within the tube and pupates (Figure 103). When the transformation is complete, the insect appears from the pupal skin as a fully developed wasp and, with its jaws, cuts open the cement door and takes to flight. Once the fully developed wasps have left the nest, you can safely examine it and observe how it was built.

There are several other species of mud daubers. The pipe-organ dauber makes a similar nest, except the tubes are divided by partitions into several chambers (Figure 104). Each chamber is provisioned with spiders and an egg is laid in each before the chamber is sealed. Another capable mason, *Odynerus*, makes a nest about the size of a hen's egg and usually attaches it to the twig of a bush (Figure 105). Perhaps the most advanced development of wasp masonry finds expression in the nests of the jug builders or potter wasps, a group of wasps that fashion their mud nests into the shape of a water jug. The nests are delightful and exquisite little objects, worthy of the skill of a master craftsman, and are about half an inch in diameter with a delicate liplike margin around the small opening, which is eventually closed (Figure 106). They are saddled on the twigs

80

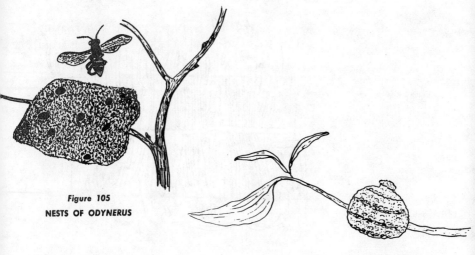

Figure 105
NESTS OF ODYNERUS

Figure 106
NEST OF POTTER WASP

of trees and shrubs. Like the nests of the daubers, they are provisioned with living food, but with caterpillars instead of spiders. If you can locate one of these nests, perhaps you can do what the famous French entomologist Fabre once did. He made a small opening in the nest and through this window was able to observe what went on inside.

ADVENTURE 14

We Become Acquainted with the Engravers

SOMETIME WHEN YOU are outdoors, pull the bark from a dead branch or trunk of a dead tree and examine the inner layer, or sapwood. Very likely you will find it ornamented with smoothly cut burrows similar to those shown in Figure 107. The burrows are the work of small or medium-sized beetles which are usu-

81

Figure 107
BURROWS OF ASH-BARK BEETLE

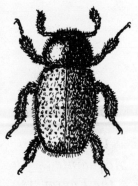

Figure 108
PEACH-TREE BARK BEETLE

ally brown but sometimes black, and generally with the hind end of the body blunt, as if cut off transversely (Figure 108). They are known as engraver beetles or bark beetles, and like the leaf miners, each species makes its own characteristic pattern of burrows.

The habits of the beetles vary greatly, but in general the female beetle, after penetrating the bark, excavates a tunnel or burrow in the inner layer of the bark or sapwood or perhaps in both. This initial burrow is known as the egg burrow and may be either simple or branched. Most species make niches in the sides of the tunnel and, as eggs are deposited in them, they are called egg niches.

82

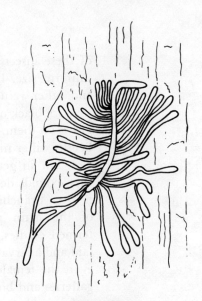

Figure 109
BURROWS OF FRUIT-TREE
BARK BEETLE

When the larvae emerge, they feed on the bark or sapwood or both, and thus fashion lateral tunnels which often extend parallel in a more or less regular manner as shown in Figure 109. Most engraver beetles infest forest trees, but a few species like the fruit-tree bark beetle and the peach-tree bark beetle attack fruit trees. The burrows of the former are shown in Figure 109.

Closely related to the engraver beetles are the ambrosia beetles, or timber beetles. They are called ambrosia beetles because they feed on the fungi which invariably grow in their burrows and timber beetles because they tunnel in solid wood. The burrows, or galleries, of these insects may be recognized by their uniform size, by the absence of wood dust and other refuse, and by the stained walls that are black or brown from the fungus that grows on them. The galleries of the ambrosia beetles differ in pattern according to the species, but in general there is a main gallery that extends deeply into the solid wood and is often branched. Extending down the sides of the main gallery are short chambers, termed cradles, in each of which an egg is laid and a larva reared. In some species, however, the female lays her eggs loosely in the galleries and both the young and old live together in the same quarters.

Where the larvae are reared in separate cradles, the mother beetle is in constant attendance upon her young during their development and jealously guards them. The opening of each cradle is closed with a plug of the food fungus, and as soon as this is consumed it is replaced with fresh material. At intervals the larvae perforate the plug and clean out their cells, pushing out pellets of excrement through the opening. The pellets are promptly removed by the mother beetle and the opening again sealed. The young transform into beetles before leaving their cradles and emerging into the galleries. The galleries are excavated only by the adult beetles. In some species the galleries are started by the female and she does all, or nearly all, the construction work. The male may enter the new burrow and perhaps assist in building a nuptial chamber or in the disposal of wastes, but as a rule his only duty is to fertilize the female. The galleries that are excavated exclusively by the female have a variety of forms—simple cavities, regular or irregular longitudinal or transverse galleries, or even forked ones.

In other species the male begins the burrow and does all of the early construction work. The initial burrow is an irregular cavity with a nuptial chamber, and when the work has progressed to this point, the female takes over and excavates separate egg galleries off the nuptial chamber. According to the species, the galleries may take a general longitudinal direction in regard to the grain of wood, or a transverse direction, or may bear no relation at all to the grain of wood, but in any case the completed burrow is more or less radiate or stellate in form. The egg galleries are usually of uniform diameter and are just large enough to permit the passage of the beetles. In instances where they are unusually long, they may have at varying distances small alcoves known as turning niches, into which the insect may back up and reverse its direction; where no such provision is made, the female must back into the nuptial chamber in order to turn around. Under favorable conditions colonies of these

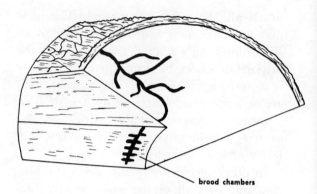

brood chambers

Figure 110
BURROWS OF APPLE-WOOD STAINER

Figure 111
LARVA OF HARRIS'S SPHINX
IN A GROUP OF PINE NEEDLES

beetles may continue their excavating activities for two or three generations. The galleries of these beetles may be classified into about ten general types, and each type usually shows considerable variation in size, direction, and position of the component parts.

Collect a number of burrows to show general patterns and get acquainted with the insects that make them. In Figure 110 are pictured the burrows of the apple-wood stainer, the name being something of a misnomer, as the insect breeds in oak, birch, beech, spruce, and pine as well as fruit trees. It sinks its slender, blackened galleries deeply into the wood, as you can see from the drawing.

MANY INSECTS MAKE use of natural cracks, crevices, holes and similar places as temporary shelters. Others occupy curled leaves or other forms of leaf distortion or may find a retreat in a bunch of leaves, like the larva of Harris's sphinx, which rests head downward in a group of pine needles (Figure 111). The leaves are not curled or drawn together but are naturally bunched, and the insect lives among them protected by its striped color pattern that resembles the pine needles. The larva of the pine-tube moth has improved on this arrangement by drawing a group of needles together and tying them with silk that it spins to form a tube in which to live (Figure 112). Since it feeds on the tips of the needles, the insect finds it necessary to make two or three such tubes during its development.

We Get To Know the Tiers, Folders, and Rollers

Figure 112
TUBE OF PINE-TUBE MOTH

Figure 113
HYDRANGEA LEAVES SEWN
BY HYDRANGEA-LEAF TIER

Other species have the same habit of tying leaves together to form a shelter. The hydrangea-leaf tier is a common insect that you can find on hydrangea shrubs. The little green caterpillar sews two terminal leaves together, enclosing the flower bud (Figure 113). The insect lives within the two leaves and feeds upon the developing flower as well as the inner surfaces of the leaves. The leaves continue to grow, however, and eventually form a bladderlike pouch. Another leaf tier, as the insects that tie leaves together are called, is the silver-spotted skipper, which may be seen on the locust tree. The larva, which is leaf-green with a brown head, makes a nest by fastening together the leaflets of the compound leaf. It lives concealed (Figure 114), emerging only to feed. Unlike tiers that construct shelters for a single occupant, the poplar-leaf tier is a gregarious insect. When the eggs, which are laid on a poplar leaf, hatch, the larvae at first tie two leaves together, between which they feed. Later they draw in other leaves and construct a larger

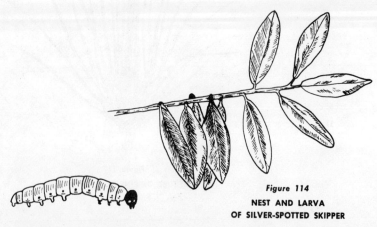

Figure 114
NEST AND LARVA
OF SILVER-SPOTTED SKIPPER

nest. Look for them any time from May to October.

A number of insects use naturally rolled or curled leaves, but others roll or fold their own. The insect first spins threads of silk across the part of the leaf to be rolled or folded. If the insect wants to roll the leaf lengthwise, it attaches the strands of silk perpendicular to the midrib of the leaf; if the insect wants to roll the leaf crosswise, it attaches the strands parallel to it. As the strands of silk dry, they shrink and pull the edges of the leaf inward. Then newer and shorter strands are spun and as these shrink, the edges of the leaf are pulled still closer together. This operation is repeated until the edges of the leaf are drawn completely over and fastened with other strands. The silk is always spun on the upper side of the leaf, as the leaf naturally bends more easily in that direction. To observe the complete operation, remove a partially developed larva from its shelter and place it on another leaf. It will immediately go to work and fashion another temporary home.

Some leaf rollers use the leaves as food. The rolled leaves of the basswood-leaf roller are conspicuous in later summer on basswood trees, and if one is examined, it will be found that the tube or roll is formed of several thicknesses of the leaf (Figure 115). Living within it is a bright-green larva with a shiny

Figure 115
BASSWOOD-LEAF ROLLER

Figure 116
LEAF ROLL
OF BUCKTHORN TORTRICID

black head and thoracic shield. It feeds upon the inner rolls of the tube and excretes numerous fecular pellets that accumulate at the lower end. The insect leaves the roll when full-grown and makes a smaller one that it lines with silk, in which it spends the winter.

The buckthorn tortricid is also a roller that feeds on its shelter. The insect makes a characteristic fold near the tip of the leaf and feeds beyond the fold toward the tip, extending the fold backward toward the base of the leaf as it continues its feeding operations (Figure 116). Other leaf rollers remain within their shelters but protrude their heads and feed upon the adjacent foliage. The dusky leaf roller, which may be found on the apple, feeds in this manner.

For some insects a rolled leaf serves as a convenient shelter when pupating. The promethea moth (Figure 117), the grape-

Figure 117
COCOON OF PROMETHEA MOTH
IN FOLDED LEAF

Figure 118
WINTER QUARTERS
OF VICEROY LARVA

Figure 119
WINTER NEST
OF BROWN-TAIL MOTH

berry moth, and the viceroy butterfly (Figure 118), make use of rolled leaves for this purpose. The larvae of the brown-tail moth make a communal nest in which they hiberate (Figure 119). An interesting sidelight in connection with the habits of leaf-rolling insects is that when they abandon their shelters, other insects often take occupancy, and certain scavengers feed upon the fecula left by the original makers. As the shelters are frequently occupied by different species, particularly in cool, damp weather, they should be included among the places to look if you collect insects.

The leaf folders do not differ from the leaf rollers except that they fold the edges of the leaves instead of twisting them into rolls. Sometimes they are known as leaf sewers. A few common species that you can look for are the apple-leaf sewer, the grape-leaf folder (Figure 120), and the rose-leaf folder, the last one a familiar insect in our gardens.

Figure 120
FOLDED LEAF OF
GRAPE-LEAF FOLDER

EXCEPT FOR THE silkworm, we usually associate the silk-spinning habit with spiders, whose webs are found throughout the summer on herbage of all kinds and throughout the entire year in our houses and cellars— the familiar cobwebs. Many insects, however, are capable of spinning silk and some of them, as we saw in our last Adventure, use

ADVENTURE 16

We Watch Some Tentmakers at Work

Figure 121
LARVA OF
SPICEBUSH SWALLOWTAIL
ON MAT OF SILK

the silk to tie leaves together for a shelter. Others use the silk to form mats, webs, tubes, and cases of various kinds. The silk insects spin is secreted either by the cephalic glands, which are elongate and coiled and open to the exterior through the lower lip, by the salivary glands, a term applied to various glands opening in the vicinity of the mouth, or by the caudal or modified Malpighian glands. The amount produced by the silk-spinning insects varies in the different species and determines the extent to which it may be used.

A few insects, like the larvae of the tent feeder, make use of the silk to spin a dense mat. This mat, spun on the lower surface of a leaf, serves as a temporary shelter. The larva of the spicebush swallowtail spins a similar mat in a folded leaf, but is not a true leaf folder since it does not actually fold the leaf (Figure 121). Other species spin large silken nests or webs. Many of them are known as leaf webbers and ugly-nest builders, terms descriptive of their habits, but actually they are leaf tiers, since their large silken nests or tents incorporate a number of leaves. The tortricids are masters at this sort of thing. The eggs are laid in compact masses, and when the larvae emerge they attack the opening buds and begin to fasten the leaves together. Sometimes they ·start by rolling individual leaves, but the result is the same—a large silken nest containing a number of leaves which eventually die and turn brown, giving the entire mass a dirty and unkempt appearance. Hence the name ugly-nest tortricids. The next time you see one, examine it (Figure 122) before the leaves have turned brown and you will find either the larvae or pupae, since the larvae pupate within the nests. The pupae, however, work themselves part way from the nests before the adult moths emerge.

Unlike the tortricids, the tent caterpillars do not make use of leaves (Figure 123) but spin tents entirely of silk. On emerging from the eggs, the caterpillars, which are gregarious, feed first on the unopened buds and later on the leaves when they expand. Sometimes

Figure 122
NEST OF OAK UGLY-NEST TORTRICID

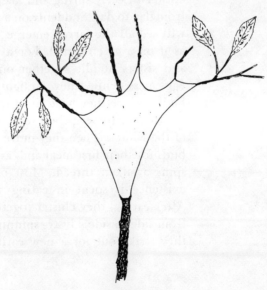

Figure 123
SILKEN TENT OF TENT CATERPILLAR

they begin their nest where the eggs were clustered on the twig or branch, but more frequently they migrate down the twig or branch toward the trunk of the tree until a large fork is reached, where they begin to spin. The reason for this is that the tent often reaches a considerable size, sometimes as much as two feet in length.

The caterpillars leave the nest daily to feed. On these feeding excursions they follow, to some extent, definite paths that may be recognized by silken threads that they spin wherever they go.

The caterpillars are most interesting to keep under observation from the moment they hatch until they leave the nest to search for a suitable place to pupate. Locate an egg cluster in early spring and keep an eye on it from day to day. Suddenly on a warm day you will see all the larvae emerge from the eggs as if on a given signal. For a time brothers and sisters huddle together on the deserted egg mass while they straighten out their bodies, since they have lived in the cramped quarters of the egg shell for the greater part of the winter. Then they move to the nearest buds for their first meal and, as they go, each spins a silken thread. Most of their larval existence is spent in eating and spinning. After eating, they cluster together and move from side to side, always spinning silk. When they strike out for a new eating place they

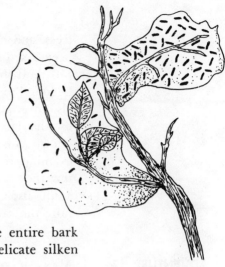

Figure 124
FALL WEBWORM

spin threads, so eventually the entire bark of the tree is covered with delicate silken carpets, on which they walk.

An interesting project would be to keep a record of how much the nest varies in size from day to day and how the growth is related to the number of caterpillars in the colony. You might even keep a comparative record of another colony and note whether the increase in size of the second nest measures the same as the increase in size of the first. If the two do not agree, perhaps you can find the reason. It may be due to a difference in the number of individuals in the two colonies, the abundance of food supply, or some other factor such as temperature, light, or some ecological condition according to the location of the food plant.

The large silken nests of the tent caterpillars appear in spring; later in the summer and early autumn similar nests appear on various trees, and one might believe that there has been a second appearance of the tent caterpillars. If these nests are examined, they will be found to be much lighter in texture. They also cover all the leaves. These nests are made by the larvae or caterpillars of an insect known as fall webworm (Figure 124). If you examine the caterpillars, you will observe that they vary greatly in their markings. The adults also vary, as you would find should you raise the caterpillars into winged moths.

ADVENTURE 17

We Hear of the Casemakers

MANY INSECTS, INSTEAD of using their silk to tie leaves together or to make a silken nest, use it to make a silken tube or to tie various materials together into the form of a tube. These tubes are known as cases, and the insects as casemakers or case-bearers. The distinction between a casemaker and a case-bearer is a fine one, for in either case the insect is a casemaker; however, some casemakers carry their cases around with them and are known as case-bearers. There are only a few species of case-bearers, and none actually makes a case that is completely portable, for all eventually fasten their cases to some support when the time comes for them to pupate.

The cases are usually cylindrical, but they may vary in form. The leaf crumplers, a name given to certain insects because they crumple the leaves, make much curved and twisted conical tubes, small at the closed end and considerably larger at the open end, that are often large and conspicuous. The larvae live within the tubes and feed on adjacent foliage, at the same time drawing the leaves in and tying them together with silk. Because of this habit they can also be considered leaf tiers; actually the casemaking habit intergrades with the leaf-rolling and leaf-folding habits, since all depend upon the insect's ability to spin silk. The apple-leaf crumpler is a common and fairly abundant insect and a typical representative of the leaf crumplers. The larvae make trumpet-shaped cases that they cover with black fecula (Figure 125). Before the end of summer the leaves are gathered together in conspicuous masses and the silken cases are hidden. In winter look

Figure 125
CASE OF APPLE-LEAF CRUMPLER

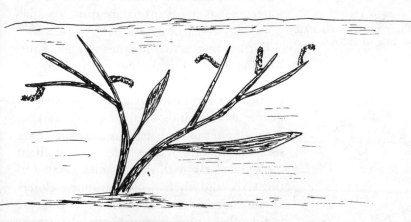

Figure 126
TUBES OF MIDGE LARVAE

Figure 127
CASE OF BLACK FLY

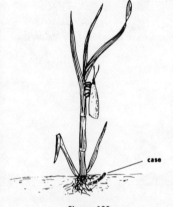

case

Figure 128
ADULT VAGABOND ON GRASS STALK
AND CASE IN GROUND

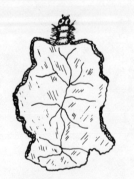

Figure 129
LILY-LEAF CATERPILLAR AND CASE

for withered, crumpled leaves on apple, plum, or cherry trees and you will likely find the cases, which will probably be still occupied by the larvae. Examine one of them and you will see how it is constructed.

The larvae of various midges live in delicate silken tubes (Figure 126) to which mud and particles of sand or vegetable matter are attached. The tubes are fastened to plants or occur in profusion on the bottoms of ponds. They may be obtained by examining a litter of dead leaves in a pool or by scooping out with a basin some of the bottom mud of the pond and letting the "catch" stand for two or three hours. The sides of the basin should then be covered with a network of tubes. The larvae of the black flies make boot-shaped cases (Figure 127) in which they pupate. These pupal cases form golden blankets on the rocks in swift streams of cold water and, as the blankets are quite conspicuous, may easily be found.

Certain insects that live in meal and flour, like the meal moth, Indian meal-moth, and Mediterranean flour moth, construct tubes of particles of meal or flour that they fasten together with strands of silk. When walking through a meadow or pasture, you may have seen small moths suddenly fly up and alight on a grass stalk with their bodies parallel to the stalk and their wings wrapped closely about their bodies (Figure 128). The larvae build silken tubes in which bits of earth or

98

Figure 130
CASE OF MAPLE CASE-BEARER

vegetable matter are incorporated. As the tubes are constructed at or below the surface of the ground, they are not easily found.

The lily-leaf caterpillar, common in quiet water among yellow and white water lilies, makes an unusual case by biting off two pieces of lily pad, each about an inch long, and fastening the edges together with strands of silk (Figure 129). Sometimes the caterpillar bites off only one piece and attaches it to the underside of the same lily pad. As the case is below the surface of the water and is filled with water, the caterpillar is provided with gills for breathing. A related species also builds a similar case, but as the insect doesn't have gills, it depends on bubbles of air that surround the case and possibly on the oxygen liberated by the bits of green leaf that compose the case.

The maple case-bearer makes a most inter-

Figure 131
CASE OF PISTOL CASE-BEARER

Figure 132
CASE OF CIGAR CASE-BEARER

Figure 133
WINTER CASE OF EVERGREEN BAGWORM

esting case. The larva cuts an oval-shaped piece of maple leaf, places it over its back, and fastens it down with silk around the edges (Figure 130). This serves as a house, beneath which it lives. As the insect eats and grows, this house becomes too small for it. At this point the insect reaches beyond the edge of the case and cuts a new oval piece, slightly larger than the first, and fastens it to the outer edges of the smaller piece. It then turns the case over so that the original or smaller case is on the leaf and the larger on its back. The larger is then fastened to the leaf. The larva rests between the two cases and feeds by protruding its head and eating the leaf tissues it can reach without leaving its case. When it has eaten all food within reach, it cuts the case loose and, carrying it on its back, moves to a new spot on the leaf. As it moves, it looks like a small turtle. The larva may change its position a number of times and the leaf, as a result, becomes perforated with a number of elliptical holes and marked by a number of ringlike patches in which the green leafy tissues have been destroyed. We have seen that when the old case gets too small, the larva cuts a new oval piece slightly larger than the first and all around the old one. This would seem to be the equivalent of sawing off a branch you are sitting on. Find out how the insect avoids such a catastrophe.

Many cases have a characteristic shape, like

100

the pistol-shaped case (Figure 131) made by the pistol case-bearer and the cigar-shaped case (Figure 132) of the cigar case-bearer. The cases are constructed of silk, pubescence from leaves, and excrement. As both insects are pests of apple, the cases are found on the apple leaves. Bagworms also make characteristic cases (Figure 133). These insects bite off pieces of bark and build them into silk-lined shelters that they further modify by attaching pieces of leaves. They carry their cases about with them until they become full-grown. Then they fasten them to a twig and pupate within them. There are several species of bagworms, but the best-known is the evergreen bagworm. It feeds on a number of trees, but prefers red cedar and arbor vitae. Its case measures about two inches long and can be found throughout the winter. It contains the eggs deposited in it by the female. However, some cases may be found empty; they are the cases in which the males developed.

Figure 134
CASE OF CASEMAKING
CLOTHES MOTH

Clothes moths are often troublesome pests. The larvae of one species, known as the casemaking clothes moth, spin cylindrical cases of silk and fragments of the material on which they live (Figure 134). If you can obtain some of these insects and place them in a covered jar containing some of the material on which they feed, you can observe with a hand lens how they enlarge their cases to accommodate an increase in size.

SOME INSECTS are able to make paper tough enough to withstand wind and rain. Yellow jackets (Figure 135), familiar to most of us, are brightly colored wasps that scrape off bits of wood from weather-worn fences or boards and convert the bits of wood into paper they use to build their nests. They generally build them in holes in the ground and enlarge them as the need arises, but sometimes they build in a stump or under some object lying on the ground. As these wasps can become very waspish at times and do not care to be disturbed, it is inadvisable to watch them while nest-building. We can, however, examine the nest when the wasps have left, after cold weather has set in, to learn how it is constructed.

The paper of which the nest is made is brownish in color and is made of partially decayed wood the insects reduce to a pulp with their saliva. At least that is what they are supposed to use and perhaps still do, although some people have found they now use man made paper, particularly cardboard posters, that they chew up and mix with their saliva.

They begin the nest by building a comb consisting of a few hexagonal cells that open downward. The comb is fastened firmly near

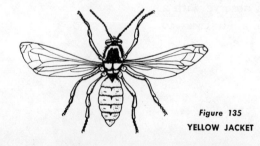

Figure 135
YELLOW JACKET

the center to a central core or axis, also of paper, that is attached at the top to the roof of the hole if built in the ground or to the lower surface of an object lying on the ground. The comb is then covered with layers made up of small overlapping shell-like sections, each firmly attached by its edges to the underlying sections.

As the wasp colony grows, the wasps enlarge the nest by adding more combs and cutting away the paper from inside the covering so they may increase the size of each comb by adding cells to the edges. To compensate for the layers removed, they build additional layers on the outside. The result of such successive combs and layers is a fairly large nest by the end of summer. Should you examine a nest, you will find that some of the later combs contain cells that are larger than those of the earlier combs. The reason is that workers are developed in the smaller combs in the spring. These workers carry on the activities of the nest until late summer, when sexual forms are produced. These are larger and therefore larger cells are made to accommodate them. When the sexual forms mature, mating takes place and provision is made to carry the species through the winter.

The extremely large paper nests that are often seen suspended from the branches of trees and shrubs are made by the white-faced hornets (Figure 136). These hornets (Figure

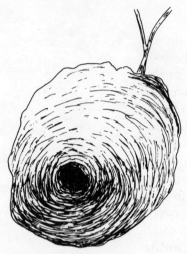

Figure 136
NEST OF WHITE-FACED HORNET

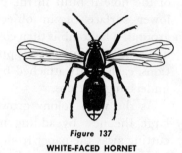

Figure 137
WHITE-FACED HORNET

137) are rather large insects and are black with a white face. Their nests are similar in construction to yellow jackets' except the paper is grayish. The paper is also stronger, and for this reason the envelope is composed of sheets of considerable size rather than small sections, as in the nests of the yellow jackets. Sometimes only a single sheet is used. These nests are so strong that they endure well into winter, even though they may be buffeted by rain, sleet, and wind.

Most of us have seen the nests shown in Figure 138 hanging beneath the eaves of buildings, in attics, and in barns and sheds. They are made by paper wasps, *Polistes* (Figure 139), uniformaly brown insects quite common in our gardens. The nest consists of a single naked comb and resembles an open

104

Figure 138
NEST OF *POLISTES*

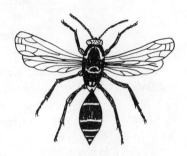

Figure 139
PAPER WASP *POLISTES*

paper umbrella without a handle, hung by
its tip. These wasps are not quite so waspish
as the others and do not seem to mind if we
approach fairly close to watch them at their
work, provided we do not molest them or
interfere with their activities. If you examine
an active colony, you will find that nearly
every open cell contains a white egg or a
chubby little soft-bodied grub. The closed
cells contain pupae in various stages of transformation. The grubs hang head-down and
are held in place by a sticky disc at the rear
end of their bodies and later by their enlarged heads, which completely fill the openings of the cells. They are constantly nursed
by the workers and fed first on the sugary
nectar of flowers and the juices of fruits.
Later they are given more substantial food,

such as the softer parts of caterpillars, flies, bees, and other insects that have been reduced to a pulp by mastication.

ADVENTURE 19

We Listen to Some Music and Learn How Sounds Are Made

THE CHIRPING OF FIELD CRICKETS is a familiar sound on summer nights. Only the males can chirp. The females lack the means of producing any sound. It was once believed that the males chirp to attract the females, but it has been shown that the females do not pay much attention to their serenades.

The best and only way to find out how they chirp is to watch them. Get one or two males (they may be distinguished from the females by the absence of an ovipositor) and watch them at close quarters. Incidentally, crickets make excellent pets and may be kept in a large jar, flowerpot–lamp–chimney terrarium, or an aquarium containing a little soil. They may be fed bits of melon and other fruits, lettuce, and moist bread. A little bone meal should also be supplied to reduce cannibalism.

When a male cricket chirps, observe that he raises his wing covers to an angle of forty-five degrees (Figure 140) and rubs them to-

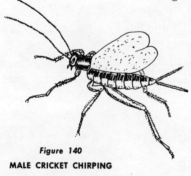

Figure 140
MALE CRICKET CHIRPING

gether. Actually there is more to it than this, for if you will examine one of the wing covers with your hand lens, you will find that the veins form a peculiar scroll pattern that serves as a framework for making a sounding board of the wing membrane by stretching it out like a drumhead. Note also that near the base of the wing there is a heavy cross vein, covered with transverse ridges, called the file (Figure 141). Next find, on the inner edge of the same wing and near the base, a hardened area. This area is called the scraper. The cricket sounds his notes by drawing the scraper of the under wing cover against the file (Figure 142) of the overlapping one. We can produce a similar sound by running a file along the edge of a tin can.

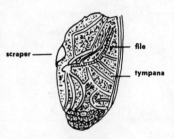

Figure 141
FOREWING OF MALE CRICKET

As the wing covers are excellent sounding boards (tympanums) and quiver when the note is made, the surrounding air is set into vibration, thus creating sound waves that can travel a considerable distance. It is interesting to note that the field cricket can alternate his use of the wing covers—that is, he can use one wing cover as a scraper and the other as a file and then reverse them. In this way he can reduce wear and tear.

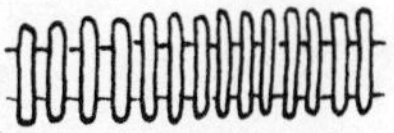

Figure 142
SECTION OF FILE

A sound-producing apparatus is not much use to the crickets unless they can hear the sounds. Whether insects can hear is a rather controversial question, although there seems little doubt that some of them can hear. We

107

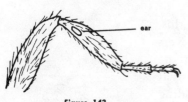

Figure 143
FRONT LEG OF FIELD CRICKET

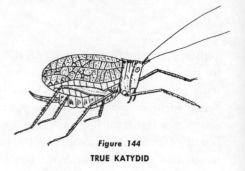

Figure 144
TRUE KATYDID

can prove this in the case of crickets by obtaining a male and female. Place the male in a small wire cage about three inches in diameter of very fine mesh, and cover one side with paper. Set the cage with the male on a table. Meanwhile keep the female in a small cardboard box which has a few small holes for air. The moment the male begins to chirp, release the female on the table but in a place where the paper wall is between her and the male. She will, if so inclined, at once move toward the male, although he is completely hidden from her. Should he stop chirping, she will become uncertain as to what direction to follow and finally come to rest. How do crickets hear? Look on the tibia of the front leg for a small white disclike spot (Figure 143); this is the ear. It is visible to the naked eye.

Male katydids (Figure 144) make sounds much the same way as male field crickets. However, the katydids are left-handed musicians, as there is a file on the left wing only (Figure 145). The file consists of about fifty-

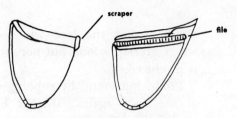

Figure 145

PARTS OF WINGS OF MALE KATYDID

five teeth. To chirp, the insect at first spreads the wing covers a little, then closes them gradually. As they close, the scraper clicks across the teeth, making from twenty to thirty sharp "tick"-like sounds in rapid succession.

A common species of grasshopper, *Stenobothrus,* makes a sound by rubbing its hind legs against the outside surface of the front wings. The femors of the legs (Figure 146) are provided with a series of pegs, called the file (Figure 147), which are scraped against the elevated veins of the wings. The two wings and femurs constitute a pair of violin-like organs, the thickened veins corresponding to the strings, the membrane of the wing to the body of the instrument, and the file of the femur to the bow. When about to play, the insect assumes a nearly horizontal position and, raising both hind legs at once, rasps the femurs against the outer surface of the wings. The Carolina locust, a familiar insect in summer in fields and meadows and on roadsides, makes a crackling sound during flight or while poising by rubbing the hind

Figure 146

FEMUR OF STENOBOTHRUS

Figure 147

PEGS OF STENOBOTHRUS

109

wings against the fore wings. Where the wings overlap a loud but not musical sound is produced.

Producing sound by rubbing one portion of the body against another is known as stridulation. Rasping organs are found in a great many insects and vary greatly in form and in their location on the body. In some beetles they are located on the head. The water boatman and the back swimmer make a clicking sound by rubbing the front legs against their proboscis. The sphingid moths sometimes produce a sound by rubbing the palpi against the proboscis. One of the powder-post beetles (Figure 148) is said to rub its front legs against a projection at the posterior angle of the prothorax. The familiar click beetles (Figure 149) make a sound by means of a spine located on the ventral surface of the body. The spine normally rests in a groove on the ventral surface of the mesothorax. The connection between the pro- and mesothorax is more flexible than in most insects. As the prothorax is flexed upward, the ventral spine slips over a sharp edge on the anterior margin of the mesothorax and produces a clicking sound. You can easily observe this by placing one of these beetles on its back. It immediately springs into the air. It does so by bending its body up and suddenly straightening it out. As it bounces up, it turns right side up, making its

Figure 148
POWDER-POST BEETLE

110

spine

Figure 149
CLICK BEETLE

characteristic clicking sound, and lands on its feet.

Although sounds are usually made by adult insects, the larva of some produce faint sounds. The most interesting example is the larva of the horned passalus, a widely distributed species in the United States. Look in decaying wood, where you should find both the adult beetle and the larva. When you examine the larva it may seem to have only four legs, but if you look closely you will see that the hind legs are minute and modified to form rasping organs. You will also observe that each coxa of the middle legs is provided with a row of fine ridges. To produce a noise the hind legs are rubbed against these fine ridges (Figure 150).

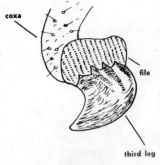

Figure 150

SOUND-PRODUCING ORGANS
OF LARVA OF PASSALUS

AS WE SAW in the last Adventure, some insects produce sound by rubbing one portion of the body against another. Others, however, create sound waves by vibrating their wings. Deathwatch beetles make a faint ticking sound by bumping their heads against the sides of their burrows. Various clicking sounds are made by certain wood-boring larvae also as they gnaw through solid wood. The minute powder-post beetles make a sound that can be heard at a distance.

The sounds made by these insects are, however, incidental sounds and are not produced

ADVENTURE 20

We Learn More about How Sounds Are Made

by specific sound-producing organs. In flies
and certain other insects sound is produced
by means of the spiracles, the external openings of the respiratory system. Behind each
spiracle is a membrane that vibrates during
respiration, as the air is being taken in and
expelled. The queen bee, the blowfly, and
the May beetle make sounds in this way.
These insects are generally called drummers,
since the sound is made by a vibrating membrane. The classical drummer of the insect
world is the cicada (Figure 151), whose sound
organs are the most complicated found anywhere in the animal kingdom. The details of the sound apparatus vary somewhat
in the different species of cicadas, but essentially it is as follows: on the underside of the
third thoracic segment of the male are two
large plates called opercula, which can be
seen quite readily and which can be lifted
slightly. Each operculum serves as a lid, covering a pair of cavities that contain the sound
organs, and probably functions as a protective
covering. The cavities are known as the ventral cavity and the lateral cavity. In the lateral
cavity is a membrane called the timbal; in
the ventral cavity are two membranes called
the folded membrane and the mirror (Figure
152). Within the body is a large air chamber
that communicates with the exterior through
a pair of spiracles.

Sound is produced by a rapid vibration of

Figure 151
CICADA

112

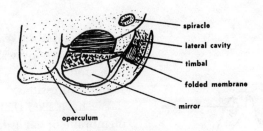

spiracle

lateral cavity

timbal

folded membrane

mirror

operculum

Figure 152

SOUND ORGANS OF CICADA

the timbal, set into motion by muscles. The other two membranes amplify the sound and the air in the air chamber acts as a resonator. In other words, the vibrations of the timbal are transmitted to the folded membrane and the mirror by the air in the air chamber, much as the strings of a piano are made to vibrate by the notes of a violin.

Since insects are capable of producing sounds, it is reasonable to suppose that they can hear, but some cannot. The females of the snowy tree cricket, for instance, have no ears and do not hear the notes of the male. However, most insects appear to have some sort of auditory organ. It is known that the antennae of the male mosquito function as a hearing organ, and it is believed that they serve a similar purpose in ants and possibly butterflies and moths. The hairs of certain caterpillars are able to pick up sound vibrations, as are the cerci of the American cockroach. Locate a cluster of tent caterpillars feeding, make a loud outcry or strike two pieces of wood together so that a sharp report

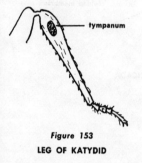

Figure 153
LEG OF KATYDID

is made, and observe the reaction of the caterpillars. The body wall itself is comparatively thin and may serve to receive numerous sound impressions.

We have seen that in crickets a tympanic membrane or ear is found on the tibia of the front legs. Similar organs are found on the front legs of katydids (Figure 153) and termites. In katydids the tympanums are oval and quite conspicuous; in crickets and termites they are sunk within the leg and only two small slits appear on the surface. The air is equalized on both sides of the membrane by special ducts that lead through the center of the leg and open on the top of the thorax. They function much like our own eustachian tubes. In short-horned grasshoppers the tympanums are located on the first abdominal segment (Figure 154) and are large and conspicuous. In water boatmen, water scorpions, the creeping water bugs, and in many butterflies and moths they are located on the thorax. See if you can find them. A vibrating membrane in itself is of no value; the vibrations of such a membrane must be transferred in some way to a nerve structure that will be affected by them if the sound is to be perceived. Such structures, called chordotonal organs, consist of rods, nerves, and nerve endings. They are complicated structures, but the morphological unit is a more or less peglike rod contained in a tubular nerve ending

114

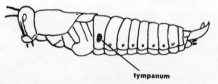

Figure 154
SIDE VIEW OF SHORT-HORNED GRASSHOPPER
WITH WINGS AND LEGS REMOVED
TO SHOW TYMPANUM

(Figure 155) which may or may not be associated with a specialized tympanum.

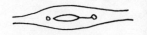

Figure 155
SIMPLE CHORDOTONAL ORGAN

WHY DO THE MALES "SING" or, for that matter, why do other insects "sing"? Does their singing serve some purpose? If it doesn't, why then are the insects provided with sound-producing organs?

In a number of cases the sound produced is incidental and the result of a normal activity. The gnawing of wood-boring larvae and the buzz and hum of flying insects correspond to the swish of a silk dress or the hum of an automobile motor. Insects such as the bee, fly, and cockroach continually clean their antennae and as they do so produce sounds that are merely incidental.

We have all heard the hum of a fly or the buzz of a bee, but how many have detected nuances in the hum or buzz? Beekeepers know that bees often buzz at different pitches. An active or vigorous bee produces note A, of 435 vibrations per second, the tired bee E, of 326 vibrations; while the spiracular tone of the same insect is at least an octave higher and often rises still higher, according to the emotional state of the insect. An experienced beekeeper is familiar with the swarming sound, the hum of the queenless colony, and the angry note of a belligerent bee, and it is likely that such notes can also

ADVENTURE 21

We Ascertain the Reasons for Insect Sounds

115

be distinguished by other members of the bee colony. It appears probable that the rate of vibration is adjusted to produce a desired note according to the occasion. This is also probably true of the note of the female mosquito, which is pitched to set the antennal hairs of the male in vibration. The notes produced by various other insects reveal similar differences, but in many cases they reflect the type of activity in which the insect is engaged rather than serving as a means of communication. For instance, those of us who have watched the mud dauber at work (see Adventure 13) have noticed that she produces a faint hum as she gathers a load of mud at the edge of a pond, but when she applies the mud to the nest the pitch is raised to a rasping sound audible at quite a distance.

That insects are able to produce sound—or more specifically, a musical note—by the vibrations of their wings, much as we produce a note by the flapping reeds of a mouth organ, seems a miracle, for in order to produce the lowest note regularly employed in music, the C of the lowest octave, the wings must vibrate thirty-two times a second, or nearly 2000 times a minute. Yet there are insects that "sing" in this way. Moreover their notes are not confined to the lower octaves. The common housefly hums F of the middle octave, and to do so must vibrate its wings 345 times a second, or 20,700 times a minute.

As a rule the note produced by the wings is constant in each species. It has been said that short-horned grasshoppers shuffle, rustle, or crackle; crickets shrill and creak; and long-horned grasshoppers scratch and scrape. Anyone, especially anyone with an ear for music, can soon become acquainted with insect "songs" and can learn to recognize the "singers" much as an ornithologist can identify a bird by its song.

Figure 156
MAY BEETLE

Undoubtedly the sounds produced by insects frequently have some purpose. We have mentioned the different notes of the honeybee and the manner in which the male mosquito locates the female. Many insects frequently frighten people by the sounds they produce. The harmless May beetle (Figure 156) is a case in point. Some insects produce a faint noise when handled—the cicada often produces a characteristic murmur when squeezed gently—and though this noise may be hardly perceptible to the human ear, it may cause birds or other animals to drop the insect. The sand cricket, when attacked, faces its enemy and boldly defies it by rubbing its hind legs vigorously against the sides of the abdomen, producing a distinct rasping noise. Since both the adults and larvae of the horned passalus live together in decaying wood, it is believed that they keep together by stridulatory signals.

Generally speaking, the sounds produced

117

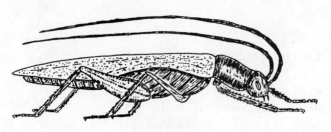

Figure 157
SNOWY TREE CRICKET

by insects are sexual calls. This is certainly true with the female snowy tree cricket (Figure 157), who responds in a peculiar manner to the singing of the male. When the male seeks his mate, he raises his wings nearly perpendicular to the body. The scraper of the left wing cover is rasped against the file on the right wing cover. When the wings are raised, a gland is exposed on the upper surface of the metathorax that secretes a liquid with a characteristic odor. The female lacks an auditory organ and cannot hear the chirps of the male, but she can detect the odor and responds to it by climbing upon the back of the male to drink the liquid secreted by the gland. As she does so, mating takes place. Thus the mating process depends not on sound signals, but on chemotropic responses.

Speaking of the snowy tree cricket reminds us that the rate of chirping in crickets depends on the temperature. During warm weather the chirp is rapid and high-pitched; during cold weather it slows down and becomes a rattle. A formula has been developed by which we can determine the temperature of the outdoors by the number of chirps per minute. For the snowy tree cricket the formula is as follows (where T equals temperature Fahrenheit, N equals the number of chirps a minute):

$$T = 50 + \frac{N - 92}{4.7}$$

For the house cricket the formula is:

$$T = 50 + \frac{N - 40}{4}$$

For the katydid the formula is:

$$T = 60 + \frac{N - 19}{3}$$

The tree cricket chirps during the day and night but is more plainly heard at night, when other sounds are not so loud. The insect is an incessant chirper and has been known to chirp 2,640 times without stopping. The snowy tree cricket is famous for another reason—it is one of the few insects that sing in chorus, since most insect musicians are soloists. Early in the evening when they begin to chirp there might not appear to be much unanimity in their chirps, but this lasts for only a short time. Soon all chirp or play in unison, and the monotonous beat of their call is continued uninterruptedly throughout the night. At times individual members of the orchestra may stop to rest, but when they resume their playing they keep time with those that have continued.

ADVENTURE 22

*We View
Some Houses*

LOOK IN THE SHALLOWER REGIONS of a pond, stream, or lake during almost any part of the summer and you will likely find what appear to be small sticks or stones moving over the bottom, presumably being carried by the water. They are not individual sticks or stones but bits of sticks or small pebbles cemented together in the form of a tube occupied by a wormlike animal. The animal is known as a caddis worm and, if all goes well, will eventually transform into a mothlike insect called a caddis fly (Figure 158).

Caddis flies are common in the vicinity of streams, ponds, and lakes and are frequently attracted to lights at night. There are a number of different species, and the larvae of most of them build houses or cases in which they live until they become winged adults. The houses are differently shaped according to

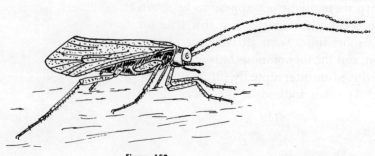

Figure 158
CADDIS FLY

the species, and are made of various materials cemented together with silk or the insects' own saliva. Some are constructed of small sticks fastened together lengthwise; some of small sticks fastened together crosswise. They look very much like miniature log cabins (Figure 159). Others are built of bits of leaves cut almost square and arranged in rings (Figure 160) or of narrow strips of leaves arranged in a spiral (Figure 161). Still others are made of pebbles with ballast stones glued on each side (Figure 162) that keep them from being carried away by the current, or of pebbles and sand grains that are cemented together in the form of a turtle-shaped (Figure 163) or snail-shaped (Figure 164) case.

Figure 159

Figure 160

Figure 161

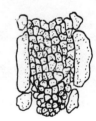

Figure 162

Figure 163

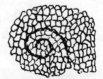

Figure 164

Figure 159-164
CASES OF CADDIS WORMS

One species makes its home of bits of rubbish and silk spun in a spiral and forming a little cornucopia (Figure 165). A few species live in hollow stems.

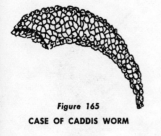

Figure 165
CASE OF CADDIS WORM

All the houses have a tough lining of silk to protect the soft-bodied caddis worms. The silk is not spun into a thread, which is customary among silk-spinning insects, but is poured forth in a gluelike sheet to which the materials that are to form the case are cemented. Each house has an opening at each end—a front door and a back door. When the insect moves about, it extends its head and six legs beyond the front door and crawls about over the bottom mud or gravel, carrying its case with it. Unlike the snail, which is attached to its shell, the caddis worm is not fastened to its case. You can easily see this for yourself by placing a case on a level surface with its occupant wrong side up and holding it by pressing down on it with your fingers. The insect will first attempt to right the case but, unable to do so, will turn itself.

If the insect is not attached to its case, how does it manage to carry its house around with it? Somewhere in its evolutionary development the caddis worm acquired two forward-curving hooks. These hooks, called grab-hooks, are located at the hind end of the body (Figure 166) and are inserted in the tough silk lining, and thus securely hold the case to the insect as it moves about.

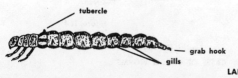

tubercle

grab hook

gills

Figure 166
LARVA OF CADDIS WORM

Caddis worms breathe by means of gills that look like short white tassels. They are attached to the sides of the worm's abdomen and are completely protected by the case. Water is made to circulate over them by undulating movements of the insect's body. Here we see the reason for the two openings in the case, as the water flows in one end and out the other. That the water may pass through the case freely, the caddis worm is provided with three tubercles that keep the case from pressing against the body.

Although we cannot watch a caddis worm build its case in its entirety, we can get some idea of how it is done by securing a vigorous half-grown larva. We remove part of its case and place the case and its occupant in a tumbler with half an inch of water and bits of its building materials. If we watch carefully, we can see how it attaches these bits to its case.

EVERYONE KNOWS that a glass prism placed in a ray of light produces a rainbow effect. A puddle in the road will do the same thing. The rainbow effect or spectrum, as it is scientifically called, is a band of colors with red at one end and purple at the other. Actually the colors we see are sensations produced in our brain by light waves when they strike certain nerve areas on the retina of the eye. Without

We Explore the Subject of Insect Colors

going into the physics of color, we can say that each color is a light wave of a definite length and frequency. Collectively the light waves that produce the colors of the spectrum compose the light we get from the sun or an electric light bulb, and if such light falls on an object, the light waves are collectively absorbed, reflected, or separated so that some may be absorbed and others reflected. If all are absorbed, the object appears black; if all are reflected the object appears white; if all are absorbed but the red wave, and this is reflected, the object appears red; if all are absorbed but the blue and this is reflected, the object appears blue; if two are reflected, a color combination is the result. There is more involved, but this is basically the idea.

To a naturalist, color is a single hue whereas coloration refers to the arrangement or pattern of colors. Some insects are drab and almost colorless; others are brilliantly colored. A few are indeed exquisite jewels, set with scales of gold and silver and etched with delicate markings. How can we explain it all?

Since color is due to the absorption or reflection of various wave lengths, the colors of insects must be due to structural peculiarities or to substances present in the skin that either absorb or reflect the waves that make up the light that falls on them. Accordingly we may classify insect colors as structural or pigmental. For instance, the green color of many caterpillars and grasshoppers is due largely to the ingestion of chlorophyll, the green coloring matter found in the leaves they eat and that tinges the blood and shows through the integument. Similarly, insects that feed on the blood of higher animals become red because of the ingested hemoglobin. Such coloring matter or substances are known as pigments. They are taken directly from the food, are manufactured indirectly from the food, or are excretory products. The brown and black colors of insects are by-products of metabolism. They are nitrogenous substances known as melanins and are diffused in the outer layer of the cuticula.

There are other pigments in the leaves beside chlorophyll, like carotene and xanthophyll, pigments that give autumn leaves their beautiful coloring. The red and yellow colors of insects are due to these pigments taken from the food plant. They occur in the cuticula and hypodermis. It is interesting to note that an insect that feeds on the Colorado potato beetle obtains its yellow from the potato beetle, which in turn gets its color from the potato leaves. A substance known as anthocyanin, which produces blue, red, and purple colors in flowers, fruit, leaves, and stems, is also responsible for the reds, purples, and possibly blues in many insects. We are doubtful about the blues, for as yet we do not know much about the blue pigments in insects. However, blue pigments are rare in insects. As a matter of fact, the blues, violets, and greens are generally structural colors. Certain other substances produce the pink, purple, and green hues in some insects. In others the red and yellow pigments are excretory products, being derivatives of uric acid. Dull yellows and browns are often derived from the tannin found in leaves.

The iridescence of a fly's wing is produced in much the same way as the iridescence of a soap bubble when light falls on it, except that the fly's wing consists of two thin, transparent, slightly separated membranes or lamellae, so that when light falls on it, it is separated into prismatic rays by the two lamellae, the color differences depending on differences in the distance between the two lamellae. The phenomenon is known as interference. The brilliant iridescent colors of a butterfly's wing are due to the diffraction of light by fine, closely parallel grooves or striae on the scales of the wings. You can see these grooves if you examine a scale with a microscope. The light is broken up by the fine grooves or ridges into its component parts much as a prism forms a spectrum. The color produced depends upon the distance between the grooves. The brilliant colors of various tropical butterflies are due, however, to the scales being both pigmented and striated. Sometimes the interference colors of butterfly scales may be due not only to surface markings, but to the lamination of the scales and to the overlapping of two or more scales. You can get some idea of how certain colors are produced by the way light is reflected by placing the wing of a bright-blue butterfly on the stage of a microscope and shading the wing so that you see it only by transmitted light from the mirror of the microscope. You will find that the blue color is absent. The reason is that the light passing directly through the scales is not broken up, and only the colors produced by the pigment are visible. Again, if you view certain scales under a microscope they are brown by transmitted light and violet by reflected light. To the unaided eye the color of the wing is either brown or violet, depending on the way the light is received, that is, from the pigment or the striated surface of the scales.

The brilliant blues and greens and iridescence in general of certain beetles are due partly to minute lines, or pits, that diffract the light. You can see these lines or pits with a magnifying glass or microscope. The pits alone, however, do not produce any color; it is only when they are combined with a reflecting or refracting surface and a pigment layer that iridescence results. The metallic sheen of many insects is produced in much the same way as the metallic luster of metals like gold, silver, or copper. These metals are extremely opaque and reflect practically all the light that strikes them. The result is the characteristic brilliant reflections. There is more to it than this, however. The distance to which light can penetrate the opaque surface of these metals is only a small fraction of a light wave. Now the depth to which different wave lengths can penetrate varies, and so some colors are transmitted more freely than others. What this amounts to is that the transmitted light is colored and the reflected light is complementary to the transmitted color. In gold the reflected light is yellow, the transmitted light blue. The greenish sheen of certain tiger beetles and wood boring buprestids is of this nature. It is all rather complicated. The silvery white color of certain insects is caused by the total reflection of light. The light may be reflected by scales, by air-filled sacs or pockets, by air-filled tracheae, or by a film of air, incorporated in the hairs of the body, that many aquatic insects such as the diving beetles carry about under water.

ADVENTURE 24

We Consider the Factors That Influence the Colors of Insects

IN THE LAST ADVENTURE we learned that in some cases insects owe their color to the food they eat—that is, their color is due directly to pigments they ingest or to pigments formed from food by chemical processes. In many instances the color of the larvae may be altered by a change in the nature of the food.

128

Even the color of the adult may be altered by a change in the larval food, other conditions being equal. Caterpillars hatched from the same batch of eggs, if separated and fed differently, may show different colors. Since little work has been done in this direction, you may want to try some experiments along this line. You must be sure, however, that the changes in color are due to changes in diet, since rapid changes in color often follow a molt—changes that are due to the development and accumulation of pigments in the hypodermis or cuticula. As a rule an insect is pale in color after molting, and within a short time a color is formed that may differ from that of the preceding instar. There is also a gradual change in color as the insect develops to maturity, and frequently an insect does not acquire its normal color until some time after it has emerged from the pupal state. Many insects may show individual color variations under exactly the same conditions. For instance caterpillars of the same brood may show variations in markings even though they may be feeding on the same plant. Locate a nest of the fall webworm and you will observe considerable variation in the markings of the caterpillars.

External stimuli such as temperature, moisture, or light often have an effect on the colors or the color pattern of an insect. The amount of heat available during the pupal

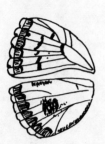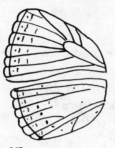

Figure 167
LOWER SURFACE OF WINGS
OF EASTERN-TAILED BLUE

spring brood   summer brood

Figure 168
LOWER SURFACE OF WINGS
OF PEARL CRESCENT

spring brood   summer brood

stage, when the pigments are forming, influences, to a large extent, the amount of pigment deposited in the wing of a butterfly. It has been shown experimentally that black or brown spots can be enlarged by exposing chrysalides to cold. If you will compare the lower surface of the wings of the spring brood of the eastern-tailed blue with the lower surface of the wings of the summer brood, you will find that the black spots of the former are considerably larger (Figure 167). The larger spots are probably the result of the chrysalides being subjected to the low winter temperatures. The variable pearl crescent shows similar differences. The lower surfaces of the wings of the spring brood are distinctly marked with blackish spots whereas those of the summer brood have very few markings (Figure 168). You can see this for yourself by chilling the pupae of the summer brood in your refrigerator. The adults that emerge from the chrysalides will be like those that appear in the spring—or some of them will be, if not all. In general the higher the temperature the brighter the coloration and, conversely, the lower the temperature the darker the coloration.

What effect moisture has on coloration, if any, is uncertain. Insular and coastal insects are somewhat darker than the inland forms, and insects found in mountain regions where the humidity is high are generally dull. Whether such color differences are due to humidity or temperature or to a combination of these factors we do not know.

Light, however, is a most important factor. Most animal pigments will not be formed without light. The seashore springtail is white upon emerging from the egg and will remain white if shielded from sunlight. When exposed to light, it assumes its normal color, black. Insects that live in the ground and wood-boring larvae are commonly white or yellow, and cave insects are generally white or pale in color. Color changes frequently occur in the eyes of certain insects to accommodate them for day and night vision; such color changes are brought about by changes in light intensity. Color changes also occur in the praying mantis and walking stick. They are usually dark at night and pale by day. Obtain one or two of these insects and you can observe these color changes. Anyone who has made an insect collection knows that certain color changes take place after the death of an insect. The eyes of certain flies lose their brilliance and the golden tortoise beetle loses its sheen. It is often necessary, if we want to preserve the color of many insects, to keep them in the dark as much as possible, but even then they lose their brilliance.

It is popularly believed that the gorgeous colors of tropical insects and the dull, monotonous colors of arctic forms are due to climatic conditions. There are, however, thousands of tropical insects that are as drab as any found elsewhere. Certain beetles found in the Temperate Zone are more brilliantly colored than members of the same family found in the tropics. Undoubtedly climate exerts a strong influence on coloration, but as yet we know too little about the effects produced by climatic factors. It has been suggested that the reason for the richer display of colors in tropical insects is due to the greater number of species and broods, hence there is a greater opportunity for color variations to develop.

Albinism, which is of common occurrence in higher animals, sometimes occurs in insects and is usually due to lack of pigment. The common yellow roadside butterfly is frequently albinic. It might be interesting to find one. Melanism is sometimes observed in insects. As far as I know, no one has yet found the cause.

Of more interest is the seasonal coloration shown by various insects. Insects that have several broods a year may have broods that differ so much from one another that anyone could easily mistake them for entirely different insects. They exhibit what is known as polymorphism, or perhaps we should say polychromism, and may be dimorphic, trimorphic, or polymorphic, depending upon the number of distinct forms. The question mark or violet-tip butterfly has two forms that differ not only in coloration but also in the form of the wings. The eastern-tailed blue has three forms: an early spring form that is small with large black markings, a later spring form that is larger with smaller black markings, and a summer form that is still larger with faint black markings. The ajax swallowtail also has three forms, each form progressively larger with longer tails to the hind wings. A number of other butterflies, such as the imported cabbage butterfly, painted lady, red admiral, tiger swallowtail, and pipe-vine swallowtail, have several forms. The seasonal increase in size is probably due to increased metabolism as a result of progressively higher temperatures, since it is well known that warmth stimulates growth, whereas cold has a retarding effect. However, some caterpillars can be so stimulated by unusual warmth that they will pupate before they are fully grown; as a result the adults are undersized. We should also point out that a butterfly need not be double- or triple-brooded to be polymorphic, since some species that are single-brooded show polymorphism. The spangled fritillary has a long brood period, extending from May to October. The butterflies that appear early in the season are smaller and duller in color than those that appear later.

ADVENTURE 25

We Do Some Collecting and Make a Surprising Discovery

IF YOU WERE TO COLLECT two specimens of the same species and compare them, you would probably find they would not be colored exactly alike. Suppose you collected, for instance, a number of specimens of the oak-leaf roller. You would discover that the moths range in color from a pale yellow to brown. Or if you collected hundreds of Colorado potato beetles (Figure 169) you would not find two with exactly the same pattern on the pronotum (Figure 170). The ilia underwing may be found in more than fifty varieties, each of which might have its own name were it not for the fact that the varieties run into each other. The wing covers of the Mexican

Figure 169
COLORADO POTATO BEETLE

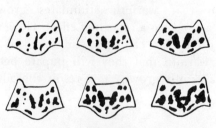

Figure 170
COLORATIONAL VARIATIONS OF PRONOTUM OF COLORADO POTATO BEETLE

bean beetle (Figure 171) show countless variations, a few of which are shown in Figure 172. Individuals of tiger beetles frequently show deviations in pattern. In many instances differences in color among specimens of the same species are slight and hardly noticeable, but they are there nevertheless.

Figure 171
MEXICAN BEAN BEETLE

Figure 172
VARIATIONS IN COLOR PATTERNS
OF ELYTRA OF MEXICAN BEAN BEETLE

Sometimes the normal color of an insect has been replaced by another. The red in the red admiral is often replaced with yellow. Ladybird beetles frequently show a replacement of color. A leaf beetle, *Lina,* is pale on emerging from the egg, but soon becomes yellow with black markings, and after several hours of sunlight the yellow changes to red. After death the red fades back through orange to yellow. Red and yellow colors are due to pigments that are closely related chemically, hence the substitution of one for another is easily made. However, the presence of a given color is usually a matter of metabolism, yellow being predominant under conditions of arrested development of pigment in the living insect. In a dead insect it is due to a process whereby the pigment is reduced.

Yellow and green pigments are similarly

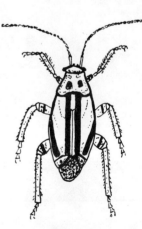

Figure 173
FOUR-LINED LEAF BUG

135

related. In the four-lined leaf bug (Figure 173), a common insect of fields and meadows, the stripes are at first yellow and later change to green. After death they again become yellow. As the green color of plant-eating insects is due to chlorophyll, the color changes from yellow to green and back to yellow are probably similar to those that occur in leaves. You have doubtless learned that leaves grown in darkness are yellow and do not become green until exposed to sunlight. In the autumn, when metabolism ceases and the leaves die, the chlorophyll disintegrates, exposing the yellow pigment xanthophyll, which has been present in the leaves but overshadowed by the more predominant chlorophyll. We must not assume, however, that all color changes are due to changes in pigment. A species of tiger beetle and one of the caterpillar hunters are frequently blue instead of green, but here the replacement of color is due to variations in the structure of the surface: Green grasshoppers sometimes turn pink toward the end of summer. Why, we do not know.

In many insects the sexes may be distinguished by differences in color. Sexual color dimorphism, better known as colorational antigeny, is best shown by the butterflies. The familiar white cabbage butterfly is a common example. The male has one conspicuous black spot on the upper side of each front

136

Figure 174

FRONT WINGS OF WHITE CABBAGE BEETLE
male   female

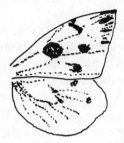

Figure 175

WINGS OF CHECKERED WHITE BUTTERFLY
male   female

wing; the female has two (Figure 174). The checkered white butterfly shows a similar colorational antigeny. The male has a few brown spots on the front wings; the female is checkered with brown on both wings (Figure 175). In the common sulphur butterfly the marginal black band of the front wings is sharp and uninterrupted in the male, whereas in the female it is diffuse and interrupted by yellow spots (Figure 176).

The sexes of swallowtail butterflies may often be distinguished by color differences. See if you can find what they are. In the butterflies known as the skippers, the males often have an oblique black dash across the middle of the front wing. The promethea moth shows color differences in the sexes. In the gypsy moth the male is olive-brown, the female white. In some species like the io moth and peach-tree borer the sexes differ remarkably. The wings of the male peach-tree borer are colorless and transparent; in

137

Figure 176

FRONT WINGS OF COMMON SULPHUR BUTTERFLY
female   male

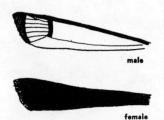

male

female

Figure 177
FRONT WINGS OF
PEACH-TREE BORER

the female the forewings are violet and opaque (Figure 177). Sometimes the same sex may show two kinds of coloration. The tiger swallowtail is a familiar example to those who are familiar with insects. In the northern states the female is yellow with black markings, in the southern states she is blackish brown with black markings.

Colorational antigeny, though more conspicuous in butterflies and moths, also occurs in other insects. The female locust tree hopper is uniformly brown in color; the male is much darker, almost black, with a conspicuous broad yellow line on each side of the body (Figure 178). The black-winged damsel fly also shows sexual differences. The wings of the male are velvety black; those of the female are smoky with a distinct white stigmatal spot on the tip of each wing. In the cherry-hawthorn sawfly the abdomen of the female is metallic black and the prothorax is rufous, whereas the abdomen of the male has a broad, whitish dorsal band and the thorax is whitish in color.

Do such sexual differences serve a useful purpose? Colorational antigeny is probably of no protective value, although coloration in general, as we shall see later, does provide the insects with a certain measure of protec-

Figure 178
SEXUAL COLOR DIFFERENCES
IN LOCUST TREE HOPPER
male   female

tion. As recognition marks whereby the sexes can locate one another, the sexual differences are in most species usually so trivial and variable as to be negligible, although in some cases they may be of value. As far as we know, insects are unable to perceive colors except in the broadest sense. Despite the great difference in the coloration of the male and female promethea moth, the male does not seek the female through color but is guided by a sense of smell. In all likelihood colorational antigeny is more accidental or incidental than a result of natural selection, and is probably due to the same conditions that produce color variations in general.

ADVENTURE 26

We Hunt with Some Hunters

THE DICTIONARY defines the word "hunt" as "to follow or search for prey for the purpose, and with the means, of capturing and killing it." Many insects fit this definition and are known as predators.

With their long legs the tiger beetles (Figures 180 and 181) can easily capture most insects they chase. The ground beetles (Figure 179) are equally predaceous. They lurk under stones and trash by day and come out at night to feed on various insects, many of which are injurious to our plants. Indeed, if we had enough of them in our gardens we would not have to worry about cutworms. Some of the larger ground beetles are known

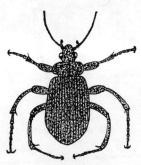

Figure 179
THE SEARCHER

139

Figure 180
TIGER BEETLE

Figure 181
LEG OF TIGER BEETLE

as caterpillar hunters, a name well taken although they feed not only on caterpillars but on other insects as well. One of them, a large, iridescent green beetle with reddish margins on the outer edge of the elytra, is known as the searcher (Figure 179). It was imported from Europe to control the gypsy and brown-tail moths.

If it were not for the ladybird beetles (Figure 182), we would have a difficult time with scale insects, plant lice, and others, for both the larvae and adults prey upon these harmful insects and devour them in great numbers. Ladybird beetles are oval or rounded in form and vary considerably in color and markings. They are generally red or yellow with black spots or black with yellow or red

140

spots. The larvae are blackish, often spotted or banded with red or yellow, and armed with distinct spines (Figure 183).

Dragonflies are also beneficial, as they prey on mosquitoes and other harmful insects, which they capture in a sort of "basket" formed by their legs. The aquatic young are also predaceous and perform the same kind of service, feeding on the larvae and pupae of mosquitoes and other insects. They are known as naiads and are quite unlike the adults (Figure 20), being dingy little creatures with six queer, spiderlike legs and no wings, although there are four little wing pads extending down the back that encase the growing wings. They have a most curious way of capturing their prey which you can see by obtaining a few of them and placing them in a small aquarium containing a layer of sand and some water plants. The aquarium should also be stocked with various water insects, such as mosquito larvae. You will observe that the naiads walk slowly over the sand, occasionally stopping to look around. When they see a likely victim they steal up to it, and suddenly the lower lip, which is hinged and has a pair of fingerlike pincers and spines, is extended outward and the prey grasped (Figure 184). Then the lip is folded back under the head and the prey conveyed to the mouth. In some species the lip covers the face like a mask (Figure 185).

141

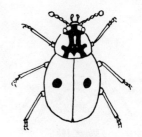

Figure 182
LADYBIRD BEETLE

Figure 183
LARVA OF LADYBIRD BEETLE

Figure 184
NAIAD OF DRAGONFLY
WITH ERECTED LABIUM

Figure 185
NAIAD OF DRAGONFLY
WITH LABIUM FOLDED

If you have ever seen a praying mantis you know how the front legs are modified for catching prey. Ordinarily this curious insect rests with its legs folded in a posture that suggests an attitude of prayer. But should an insect come within easy reach, the legs snap out quickly and suddenly and the luckless victim is seized and held firmly by the strong spines with which the tibia and tarsus are armed (Figure 186). Sometimes the mantis will not wait for an insect to come within reach but will stalk its prey, moving slowly and deliberately toward it; then, without warning, the prey is caught as in an unfailing steel trap. As soon as the prey has been caught, the mantis begins to feast, the mandibles opening a gaping hole in the soft flesh of the victim. The meal over, the mantis customarily cleans the spines on its legs and is ready for the next victim. Mantids crawl about on the foliage of trees and shrubs and frequently invade our gardens. The next time you see one, watch it for a while—or better,

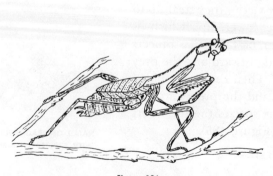

Figure 186
PRAYING MANTIS

transfer it to a terrarium, add a few insects of various kinds, and observe it at your leisure.

Another insect whose front legs are modified for grasping and which you should examine is the ambush bug (Figure 187). This insect conceals itself in flowers and lies in wait for an insect, often much larger than itself, to come within reach. The coxa of the front legs is somewhat elongated, the femur is greatly thickened so that it is half or two thirds as broad as it is long, and the tibia is sickle-shaped; the latter fits closely upon the broadened and curved end of the femur. Both the tibia and femur are armed with a series of close-set teeth, so that an unlucky victim is held as firmly as if between two saws.

Figure 187
AMBUSH BUG

Certain species of scorpion flies, found among rank herbage growing on the banks of shaded streams and in damp woods where there is a luxuriant undergrowth, have their hind legs modified for grasping insects. The front legs of the water scorpions (Figure 188) are also fitted for seizing prey, as are the front legs of the giant water bugs (Figure 34). These latter are highly rapacious, feeding on insects, snails, and small fish.

Water tigers, the larvae of the diving beetles, have jaws that are sickle-shaped and hollow with openings at the tips. When a water tiger catches sight of a promising meal, it rears up and stands at rigid attention with

Figure 188
WATER SCORPION

143

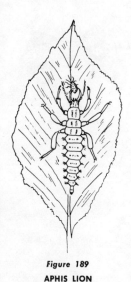

Figure 189
APHIS LION

its mandibles wide open. When the unsuspecting victim comes near, the water tiger lunges forward and clutches it between its jaws. Then, holding on firmly, it sucks the body fluids of its prey.

The jaws of the aphis lion (Figure 189) are similarly shaped. The mandibles and maxillae are slightly grooved and fit together to form a hollow tube with an opening at each end and through which liquid food is sucked. Watch a "lion" as it seizes an aphid with its pincerlike jaws, then lifts it high in the air and drinks in the green blood until the aphid is nothing but a shriveled-up skin.

A close relative, the ant lion, does not search for its prey but digs a circular pit and lies in wait at the bottom for an unsuspecting insect to fall in (Figure 190). The ant lion is a queer-looking insect with mouth parts like the aphis lion, so that the body fluids of the prey can be conveyed to the mouth—or, more strictly speaking, to the throat, since the insect does not have a mouth in the true sense of the word.

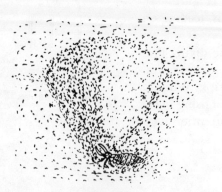

Figure 190
ANT LION IN PIT

Find an ant lion—the conical pits are made in sandy and crumbly soil protected from rain and wind—and transfer it together with some of the soil to a shallow box or dish and watch how the pits are dug. You will find it most interesting. Note whether the insect moves clockwise or counterclockwise when digging. Since ant lions have to lie in wait for their meals, days and even weeks may pass before they eat. Under such conditions two or three years may be required to reach maturity. If you care to follow their development, feed them regularly and before long they will spin a cocoon just below the surface of the sand. Eventually the adults will appear, and unless you know what adult ant lions are like, you will be surprised. They do not resemble the larvae at all.

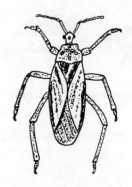

Figure 191
MASKED BEDBUG HUNTER

Assassin bugs, a group of rather striking insects, are also highly predaceous, preying on cutworms and other harmful insects. A familiar species is the masked bedbug hunter (Figure 191), so called because it often enters houses to feed on bedbugs. Another familiar

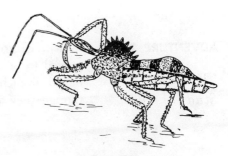

Figure 192
WHEEL BUG

Figure 193
ROBBER FLY CARRYING PREY

Figure 194
ROBBER FLY

ADVENTURE 27

*We Make a
Study of Galls*

species is the wheel bug, which has a cog-wheel crest on the prothorax (Figure 192). You should have no difficulty finding both of these insects.

Common in open fields, robber flies may often be seen swooping down upon insect victims in mid-air (Figure 193) or snatching them from leaves and carrying them away to a convenient place where they suck the body juices of their prey at their leisure. Robber flies (Figure 194) are large insects, extremely predaceous, with an elongate body and a very slender abdomen, although some species are quite stout and resemble bumblebees. They attack not only other flies but such powerful insects as bumblebees, tiger beetles, and dragonflies.

There are countless other predators, such as the water boatmen, back swimmers, dobson flies, and alder flies. Some of the stinkbugs, most of which are plant feeders, prey on other insects. Many wasps capture other insects and spiders, with which they provision their nests. Some of them are known as spider hunters. The cicada killer is the largest and perhaps the most famous of these wasps.

IN WINTER YOU have doubtless seen what appeared to be dried apples hanging from the naked branches of trees (Figure 195). Although they are called apples—more specifi-

146

cally oak apples, since they are found only on oak trees—they are not apples at all.

They are a peculiar kind of outgrowth or excrescence called a gall. Galls are found on a variety of plants, being especially numerous on the willows, oaks, roses, legumes, and the composites, and number over a thousand different kinds in North America alone. They occur on almost any part of the plant: buds, leaves, petioles, flower heads, stems, bark, and roots. They are generally caused by living organisms like fungi, nematode worms, mites, and insects. In a few instances they may be the result of mechanical irritation. They vary greatly in form, are frequently colorful, often grotesque, and sometimes conspicuous. Any given kind of gall is always made by the same kind of organism and always on the same kind of plant and on the same part of the plant. This makes it easy for anyone versed in gall lore to identify its maker.

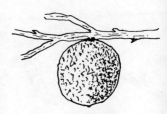

Figure 195
OAK APPLE

We do not know what causes a gall to form or why any particular kind of gall should have a distinctive form. The egg of a gall-making insect is laid upon the host plant or inserted in the tissues. When the larva emerges, it makes it way to the growing meristematic tissues—that is, on cells that are capable of dividing and multiplying—because galls are formed only on such tissues. Hence galls are the result of cell multiplication and cannot occur on a stem or leaf or

147

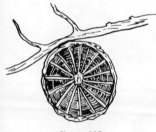

any part that has become mature. Once the larva has reached the growing tissues, a gall begins to form. The stimulus for gall formation is probably a secretion from the larva; at least that is what we believe, for the physiology of gall formation is still obscure. As it develops, the gall forms a starch that is changed to sugar by an enzyme secreted by the larva in the same way as the enzyme of the plant normally changes starch to sugar. The sugar is used by the plant to form cells and tissues that in turn are utilized by the insect as food. As more food material is produced than the insect can possibly use, the excess stimulates the cells to greater activity and to multiplying more than they would normally. The result is an abnormal outgrowth. It all seems complicated, although when we know the answer it may be a simple one.

Examine an oak apple in summer when it is still green. You will find it is firm and tough in texture. Cut it open. The interior is composed of a spongy, filamentous or corky mass and in the very center there is a cell with definite, firm walls occupied by a small, soft, juicy grub (Figure 196). Here indeed is shelter, with plenty of food and security against predators and parasites. When winter comes, examine an oak apple. You will find it thin-skinned, almost parchmentlike, easily crushed, and with a small hole through which

Figure 198
OAK SPANGLES

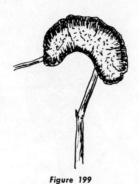

Figure 199
BLUEBERRY KIDNEY GALL

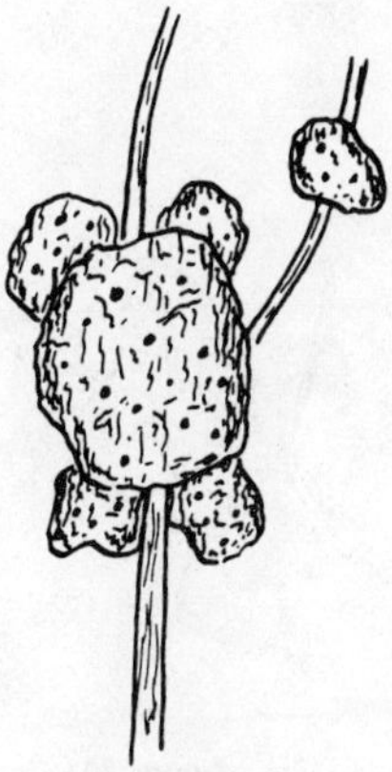

Figure 200
GOUTY OAK GALL

the adult insect escaped, which in this case was a wasp. Instead of the spongy, filamentous or corky mass, nothing remains but a series of radiating filaments supporting the central cell (Figure 197).

Galls vary considerably in shape and size. Some are very shallow, like the blister or spot galls found on asters and goldenrods. They are usually oval, flattened thickenings in the leaf surface and may measure from one-quarter to one-half inch in diameter. The spangle galls (Figure 198) are thicker and look like shallow saucers. Some galls are quite woody, like the blueberry kidney gall (Figure 199) and the gouty oak gall (Figure 200). A few galls are conical, like the witch-hazel cone gall (Figure 201). It is green or green-and-reddish-tipped and occurs on the leaves.

Figure 201
WITCH-HAZEL CONE GALL

Figure 202
SPINY ROSE GALL

Figure 204
OAK FIG GALL

Figure 205
OAK BULLET GALLS

Figure 203
COCKSCOMB ELM GALL

There are even spiny galls like the spiny rose gall (Figure 202). It is a many-spined, green or reddish, somewhat globular gall and develops on the twigs. It occurs on our garden roses. Very often a gall has a form that reminds us of some object or a structure on an animal, like the cockscomb elm gall, which resembles the comb of a cock (Figure 203). It is an irregular but comblike greenish, red-tipped elevation formed on the veins of an elm leaf.

Some galls, like the oak fig gall (Figure 204), are quite common. It occurs on the leaf stems and small twigs of white and scrub oaks in midsummer. Bullet galls (Figure 205) may frequently be seen on various oaks. Maple

150

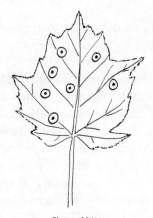

Figure 206
OCELLATE MAPLE-LEAF GALL

Figure 207
GOLDENROD BALL GALL

leaves are sometimes thickly spotted with circular eyelike spots about three eighths of an inch in diameter. This gall is known as the ocellate maple-leaf gall and is a most attractive gall with a yellow disk and margin and cherry-red central dot (Figure 206). During the winter two galls that serve as winter quarters for their makers are rather conspicuous on goldenrod stems. One is spherical (Figure 207) and encloses the hibernating maggot of a fly. The other is spindle-shaped (Figure 208) and harbors the pupa of a moth. This gall has an interesting sidelight. When the caterpillar attains its full growth and just before it changes into a pupa, it cuts a little oval opening at the upper end of the gall and fills it

Figure 208
ELLIPTICAL GOLDENROD GALL

151

Figure 209
WOOL SOWER

Figure 210
PINE-CONE GALL

with a little plug of debris. It then pupates and remains within its winter home until the following spring. At that time the fully developed moth emerges from its pupal skin, pushes its head against the plug, which falls out, and escapes into the world. Of all our galls the most distinctive is the wool sower, a white, pinkish-marked woolly growth one to one and one-half inch in diameter that encircles the twigs of the white oak (Figure 209). Made by a small wasp, it is conceded to be one of the most beautiful objects in nature, the delicate creamy white admirably set off with blotches of bright pinkish red.

Galls are easily collected and preserved and make an interesting collection. Rearing their makers, too, is absorbing and not difficult. All we need do is remove the twig or leaf or other part of the plant where the gall is formed and place it in a terrarium with the cut end of the leaf or twig placed in a bottle or vial of water so it may be kept fresh. The study of gall insects is, however, beset with certain difficulties, for we do not always know whether the insect that emerges from it is the one that made it. Many species do not make galls themselves, but lay their eggs in galls made by other species. Such guest insects are called inquilines. Furthermore, both gall makers and inquilines are attacked by parasitic insects, making the interrelations of the insects difficult to determine. The pine-cone

152

gall, a veritable insect apartment house, is a good example (Figure 210). This particular gall has been studied in considerable detail and has been found to contain, in addition to its maker, as many as thirty-one different species represented by ten inquilines, sixteen parasites, and five transients. But don't let this discourage you. Rearing gall insects can still be a lot of fun.

ADVENTURE 28

We Search for Insects in Hidden Places

TUCKED AWAY IN various parts of plants many insects live a larval existence undetected until they have left and telltale holes remain to show where they have lived. Frequently deposits of frass or sawdust pushed out through the bark indicate their presence. Or perhaps a wilting of the leaves or a shriveled stem tip may be a sign that an insect has found living quarters within the plant.

Insects that live within a plant are called borers. This may seem a contradiction, for we have found that those that live within the tissues of a leaf are known as miners (see Adventure 12). Actually there is little difference between a borer and a miner except that a borer lives deep within the tissues of a plant, whereas the miner lives just below the surface. Sometimes a boring insect may become a miner for a time. The codling moth typically bores in fruit (Figure 211) but often comes to the surface and mines for a short

Figure 211
BURROWS OF CODLING MOTH
IN APPLE

153

Figure 213
WOOD-BORING LARVA

Figure 212
SURFACE MINE OF CODLING MOTH
IN APPLE

distance just below the skin (Figure 212). You can see this if you can find some infested apples. Certain flies also show habits that intergrade between mining and boring. One of them tunnels equally well in the petioles and flower stalks as in the leaves of the dandelion.

Boring insects are essentially immature insects and are typically cylindrical in form, without legs, with reduced antennae, and with the head telescoped within the thorax (Figure 213). They are usually white or cream in color, although a few species like the hop borer and the leopard moth (Figure 214) are distinctly spotted. When the young have completed their development and have changed to adults, they usually leave the tunnels and burrows. The adults of some species of beetles spend a large part of their time in burrows and are modified somewhat to permit them to live in such an environment.

The borers are probably the most destructive of all insects because their presence is not suspected until the damage has been done and because they are difficult to control, hid-

154

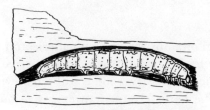

Figure 214
LARVA OF LEOPARD MOTH

den as they are beneath the surface of the plant where it is usually impossible to destroy them with poisons. They attack a great variety of plants, boring into buds, leaves, stalks, fruits, seeds, and roots—in fact, no part of the plant is immune (Figure 215). Entomologists divide them into two groups according to their nutrition: those feeding on living tissues and those feeding on dead or decaying tissues. The first group includes those that bore into buds, leaves, stalks and the like. Their food is similar to that of other plant feeders and consists of protein and soluble carbohydrates. The second group includes those that tunnel into the non-living parts like the pith and dry and decayed wood. We know very little about the nutrition of these insects. Some of them, like termites, depend on protozoa to convert cellulose into available food, while others, like certain crane flies, the long-horned beetles, and the metallic wood borers or buprestids, live in symbiotic partnership with various organisms that render their food assimilable. Other insects, like the ambrosia beetles, cultivate

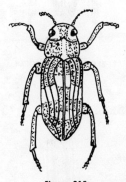

Figure 215
FLAT-HEADED APPLE-TREE BORER

155

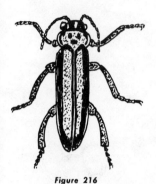

Figure 216
BRONZE BIRCH BORER

Figure 217
EUROPEAN CORN BORER

fungi or ambrosia in their galleries, on which they feed. But how some insects derive nourishment from dry wood is still unknown.

The borer group is an extensive one and includes a great many species whose habits vary widely. Wood boring is conspicuously the habit of the long-horned beetles and buprestids. Powder-post beetles, deathwatch beetles, and timber beetles are typical borers. A few caterpillars, like those of the leopard moth and the carpenter worm, bore into wood. Few flies have the wood-boring habit and only certain sawflies, such as the pigeon tremex. Insects that tunnel into twigs, like the peach-twig borer, red-necked cane borer, and the bronze birch borer (Figure 216) might be classed as wood borers, since twig boring is considered a special type of wood boring. The pruners and girdlers, like the oak pruner and the currant girdler, might also be classed as wood borers.

Insects that burrow into stalks are numerous and include many injurious species. Many of us are familiar with the European corn borer (Figure 217) and the squash-vine borer

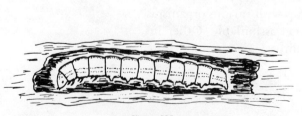

Figure 218
SQUASH-VINE BORER

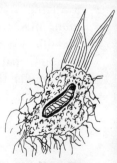

Figure 219
IRIS BORER

(Figure 218). The wheat stem sawfly is a major pest of wheat. The roots of iris and columbine plants are frequently attacked by the iris borer (Figure 219) and the columbine borer. Some of the most serious pests of fruit, such as the apple (Figure 220) and cherry maggots, the oriental fruit moth, the plum curculio, and the codling moth excavate tunnels in fruit. Most of us have at some time bitten into a wormy apple. The curculios (Figure 221) are the outstanding borers of nuts. Insects that bore into seeds fall into two groups, according to whether they feed on green or living seeds or on dry seeds. The apple-seed chalcid and the clover-seed chalcid (Figure 222) are representative of the first group; the bean weevil (Figure 223) of the second. Among the insects that burrow into buds, the eye-spotted bud moth (Figure 224) and the white-pine weevil are common examples. Lastly there are the insects that burrow into fungi. Most of these are flies and beetles.

The burrows or tunnels of the borers are characteristic of a species and serve as a clue to the identity of the burrower. Numerous

Figure 220
MAGGOTS AND BURROWS
OF APPLE MAGGOT

Figure 221
HOLE MADE IN ACORN
BY ACORN BORER

Figure 222
HOLES MADE IN CLOVER SEEDS
BY CLOVER-SEED CHALCID

Figure 223
HOLES MADE IN BEAN
BY BEAN WEEVIL

Figure 224
HOLE MADE IN BUD
BY EYE-SPOTTED BUD MOTH

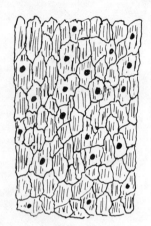

Figure 225
EXIT HOLES OF SHOT-HOLE BORER

small, shotlike holes in the bark (Figure 225) are characteristic of the shot-hole borers, and shallow engravings on the inner surface of the bark that extend into the wood are the work of engraver beetles (Figure 107). Larger and more irregular cavities in the bark, extending into the wood, are often tunnels of the buprestids, while deeper cavities are usually made by long-horned beetles and the larvae of the leopard moth (Figure 214).

The character of the frass—the refuse left by the insects and the manner in which it is disposed of—also frequently serves as a means of identifying the various species. The old-house borer pushes out to the exterior tiny pellets and fine, powdery material; the oak borer, large quantities of a fibrous material (Figure 226); the locust borer excelsiorlike borings. The round-headed apple-tree borer (Figure 227) cuts chips; the powder-post beetles produce meal-like borings; and the ants a frasslike sawdust.

Two problems confront the borers; one

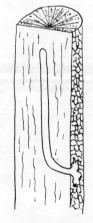

Figure 226
GALLERY OF RED-OAK BORER
SHOWING FRASS

Figure 227
FRASS PRODUCED BY ROUND-HEADED
APPLE-TREE BORER

Figure 228

**BLACK CARPENTER ANT
DISCARDING SAWDUST**

is frass disposal, the other emergence. Borers
have solved the first problem by packing the
waste at one end of the burrow, by pushing it
out to the exterior with their heads, or by
carrying it out. We often see carpenter ants
issuing from their galleries with loads of sawdust which they deposit some distance from
the entrance (Figure 228). Borers have solved
the problem of emergence in various ways
also. Perhaps you can find out what they are.
As a matter of fact, the boring insects have
many interesting habits and life cycles and to
anyone interested in entomology offer a fertile field for investigation.

CUT OFF SEVERAL dead twigs from sumac,
elder, or bramble and split them lengthwise.
In at least one of them you should find a
tunnel down the center, partitioned off as

ADVENTURE 29

*We Come upon
Some Carpenters*

159

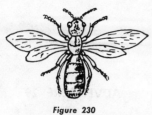

shown in Figure 229. The partitioned tunnel is an insect apartment house and is built by the little carpenter bee (Figure 230), a small, beautiful bee with a metallic-blue body.

In June or July the female bee searches for the broken twig of a bush. The reason she looks for a broken twig is that such a twig gives her access to the soft pith, which she digs out with her mandibles. When she has excavated a smooth tunnel several inches long, she stops digging operations and collects some pollen and nectar. She changes the pollen and nectar into a sort of paste called beebread and fills the bottom of the tunnel with it to a depth of about a quarter of an inch. She then lays a tiny white egg on it. Next she gathers a few chips of the pith that she has dug out and, by gluing them together, builds a partition across the tunnel above the mass of beebread. The partition forms the roof of the first cell and the floor of the one above it. On the floor of the second cell she places some more beebread, lays another egg, and builds another partition. She continues this procedure until she has filled the tunnel with cells, each one containing beebread and an egg. She does not fill the tunnel completely, but leaves a space at the end to serve as a home for herself until her family has grown up.

The first egg hatches first. The grub feeds on the beebread until full-grown, then

160

pupates, and after a while emerges from the pupal skin as an adult bee. The bee immediately begins to tear down the partition serving as the roof of its cell, but when this has been accomplished it has to wait patiently for the occupant of the cell above to transform into an adult bee. This bee in turn tears down the partition of its cell and so the procedure is repeated by each successive bee until all have transformed. The partitions removed, the remains of the partitions are pushed down the tunnel by the bees and accumulate at the bottom. When all the grubs have become adult bees they rest for a while, packed together facing the open end of the tunnel, or rather the cell occupied by the mother bee, who sits facing them. Then on a bright sunny day she leads them forth into the sunshine.

They do not, however, abandon the nest. After a while they all return and remove the remains of the partitions and other refuse from the tunnel, the old bee and the young ones working together. Then the tunnel is used again by one of the bees. Should the brood be a late one, that is, mature in the fall, the bees make use of the tunnel as a winter home. If you want to know what goes on in these nests, open them at different times of the year.

In early spring large black bees that resemble bumblebees in size and appearance

may be seen hovering about unpainted buildings. They are easily distinguished from bumblebees because the latter are more hairy, are often clothed with yellow-and-red hairs, and have pollen baskets on their hind legs. Occasionally these bees will enter a house through an open window and announce their presence with a low musical note. Later in the summer they frequently visit flowers in search of nectar and pollen.

These large bees, known as the large carpenter bees (Figure 231), build a nest similar to that of the small carpenter bee except that they tunnel in solid wood such as beams and timbers. They begin their nest by excavating a short tunnel about a quarter of an inch in diameter and less than an inch in length. At right angles to this tunnel they excavate a longer tunnel sometimes reaching a foot in length (Figure 232). Then they build successive chambers, separating them by partitions of wood chips securely cemented together and arranged in a closely wound spiral that they fill with a paste of pollen and nectar, on which they lay an egg.

Figure 232
BURROW OF LARGE CARPENTER BEE

162

The next time you see large black ants entering or leaving a dead tree or log in an almost steady procession, break open the tree or log and you will find the galleries excavated by these insects. You will observe, if you examine the galleries carefully, that they form a rather complicated series of parallel, concentric chambers. Indeed, if you can find a fairly old nest you may find a veritable labyrinth of galleries, halls, and rooms (Figure 233). You may also find a somewhat crude arrangement of the rooms into stories and half stories. The floors will probably be uneven but substantially on the same level. The galleries, or corridors or halls, will be in parallel series of two, three, or more, separated by columns and arches or by partitions cut very thin. You may also find triangular, hollow chambers. Entrance to the nest may be by circular and oblong doors that open, for the most part, into tubular, circuitous galleries communicating with the interior. Some even enter immediately upon spacious vestibules.

The white ants or termites also excavate tunnels in wood—in stumps, fence posts, logs and timber lying on the ground. Their galleries, or tunnels, run parallel to one another (Figure 234) and usually with the grain of the wood, but do not form such an intricate series of tunnels and chambers as found in the nest of the carpenter ant. The galleries or

Figure 233
GALLERIES OF
BLACK CARPENTER ANT

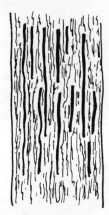

Figure 234
GALLERIES OF TERMITES

163

tunnels of the termites may be distinguished from those of the ants or other tunnel-making insects by the fact that the galleries are plastered with a grayish, mortarlike substance composed of excrement.

ADVENTURE 30

We Turn Our Attention to Cocoons

IN ADVENTURE 6 I mentioned briefly the cocoon of the cecropia moth. It is shaped like a hammock and bound firmly to a twig. The next time you find one, examine it closely. It is a tough, waterproof structure with two walls. The exterior wall is thick and made of tough, paperlike silk; the inner one, also of silk, is thinner but equally as tough. Between the two are many loose strands of silk with innumerable air spaces that provide excellent insulation. Altogether the cocoon is an admirable winter shelter, protecting the helpless pupa against moisture and sudden changes of temperature and from most birds, though the downy woodpecker frequently punctures it. It is also cleverly constructed in another respect: when the caterpillar makes its cocoon, it spins the silk at one end lengthwise instead of crosswise, thus forming a valve through which it can escape as an adult moth in the spring.

Watch the caterpillar fashion its cocoon if you possibly can. It first attaches a few strands of silk to the twig to serve as a framework.

On these supporting strands it spins a few more strands into a loose network. Once this network is in place, the caterpillar begins to spin in earnest. It works industriously and after a short time is completely screened by the silk. Finally, when the inner wall has been completed, the caterpillar changes to a pupa, at the same time secreting a substance that gives it a hard, shiny surface.

The cecropia moth is one of a group of moths known as the giant silkworms. The leaf-covered cocoon of the promethea moth, another member of the group, is a familiar sight in winter. When the caterpillar is about to spin its cocoon, it selects a leaf and covers the upper side with silk. Next it covers the petiole and fastens it to the twig with a strong band of silk, tying it so securely that the most violent winds of winter cannot dislodge it. Then it draws the two edges of the leaf together and within the folded leaf spins its cocoon. Many of us see the cocoons in winter but pass them by, thinking they are merely dead leaves hanging from the twigs. Even the most observant birds fail to detect them.

Unlike the cecropia and promethea moths, which bind their cocoons to twigs, the luna and polyphemus moths, also members of the tribe, spin their cocoons among leaves. As a result, they sometimes fall to the ground and are not often seen. The cocoon of luna (Fig-

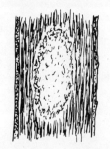

ure 235) is thin and papery and contains little silk; that of polyphemus (Figure 236) is more dense, but otherwise they are much alike. After the cocoon has been spun, the larva of polyphemus secretes a gummy, resinous substance and spreads it all over the inside. This hardens into a white, chalky coating.

In late May or early June the tent caterpillars may be seen crawling over the ground, seeking a place to pupate. They spin small tough, silken, oval cocoons dusted with a yellow powder in a sheltered nook (Figure 237). They are quite common and you can find them almost everywhere, in cracks and crevices and similar places. In contrast to these trim little cocoons, the peach-tree borer spins a rather unkempt long, oval, brown cocoon of silk and particles of bark and frass (Figure 238). The cocoon is attached to the trunk of the peach tree or built on the ground. The cocoon of the puss caterpillar is a rather unusual structure, since it has a hinged lid to permit the escape of the winged moth. It is a tough, oval affair and is usually fastened to a twig (Figure 239).

Cocoons vary considerably in size, color, shape, and materials—indeed there seems no limit in variation. Some of them are spun singly, others in clusters, and they may be constructed in almost every conceivable location. Consider the cocoon of the apple buc-

166

culatrix. It is fairly long and slender and strangely ribbed (Figure 240). Moreover the cocoon often occurs in large numbers, side by side, on the twig of an infested tree. It is these cocoons that usually first reveal the presence of the insect in an orchard. During the winter, when the leaves are off the tree, they may readily be found. Some cocoons are compactly made, others, like those of the satin moth, are loosely woven structures. Cocoons are usually thought of as egg-shaped or oval; that of the grape-leaf skeletonizer is a flattened affair. Frequently foreign materials are incorporated with the silk. We have already mentioned the cocoon of the peach-tree borer; another is the cocoon of the common maple borer. It is a small structure of silk and pellets of excrement interwoven upon the surface. Many insects that pupate in the ground incorporate particles of soil with the silk. Most caterpillars have a preference when it comes to finding a place to spin their cocoons. The caterpillars of the brown-tail moth do not seem to have any preference, for they will spin their cocoons among leaves at the tips of twigs, in crevices in bark, and in various sheltered places.

Silken cocoons are not by any means a monopoly of moths. They are also constructed by caddis worms, ant lions, aphis lions, and by the larvae of some beetles, cer-

Figure 238
COCOON OF PEACH-TREE BORER

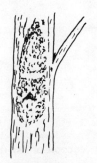

Figure 239
COCOON OF PUSS CATERPILLAR

Figure 240
COCOON OF APPLE BUCCULATRIX

Figure 241

COCOON OF YELLOW-SPOTTED
WILLOW SAWFLY

Figure 242

COCOON OF ANT LION

tain flies, and several species of sawflies. The yellow-spotted willow slug, a sawfly, spins a dark-brown cocoon at or near the ground, where it is not easily seen since it blends with the soil (Figure 241). Two other sawflies, the elm sawfly and the larch sawfly, construct tough silken cocoons in the duff or debris on the ground where they can be found only by careful searching. Many caddis worms build silken cases, as we have seen, and when the time comes for them to pupate they may alter their cases by changing the form and materials. But whether they do or not, all of them partly close their cases to keep out intruders and silt; hence their cases become cocoons. Ant lions remain in their pits when they are about to transform, and there spin a spherical cocoon (Figure 242) of sand grains fastened together with silk and neatly lined with the same material. Aphis lions also spin spherical cocoons, but theirs are made entirely of silk (Figure 243). They are attached to the lower surfaces of leaves or stems of plants. Cocoons cannot be considered beautiful objects no

Figure 243

COCOON OF APHIS LION

matter how cleverly they are made, with one exception—that spun by the spongilla fly, *Climacia*. It is made of hard, tough silk and is covered with a delicate, netlike veil (Figure 244). Although most cocoons are made of silk, many wood-boring larvae make cocoons largely of wood chips. Hairy caterpillars use silk only as a means of holding together the hairs of which the cocoon is actually made.

Emergence from the pupa, known as eclosion, is not a simple matter. Insects with chewing mouth parts merely gnaw their way to freedom, but insects with sucking mouth parts have to find some other means of escape. Some insects secrete a liquid that softens the silk at one end of the cocoon and then, by forcing the threads apart or by breaking them, make an opening. The pupae of some silkworm moths are provided with a pair of large, stout black spines with which to slit the cocoon. The pupa of the white-blotch oak-leaf miner has, at the anterior end, a toothed crest (Figure 245). The cecropia and promethea moths construct a valvelike structure at one end of the cocoon, which separates easily when the adults are ready to emerge. Even more astounding is the provision made by the puss caterpillar. Just before changing to a pupa, the caterpillar constructs near one end of the cocoon a hinged partition that serves as a trap door through which the adult emerges (Figure

169

Figure 244
COCOON OF CLIMACIA

— toothed crest

Figure 245
PUPA OF WHITE-BLOTCH
OAK-LEAF MINER

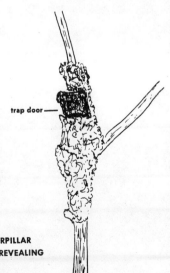

trap door—

Figure 246
COCOON OF PUSS CATERPILLAR
SHOWING LID OPEN AND REVEALING
TRAP DOOR

246). The pupa of the aphis lion cuts a circular lid from one side of the cocoon with its mandibles. After emerging from the cocoon, the pupa crawls about for a while before changing to the adult.

MANY MOTHS AND other insects fashion a covering of silk or other material as a covering for the pupa. It is designed to protect the helpless and delicate pupa from enemies, excessive moisture, sudden changes in temperature, mechanical shock, and other adverse influences. Most insects do not go to such lengths. Butterflies pupate without any protective covering and do so in exposed places. Other insects, however, seek some sheltered place, perhaps beneath the bark of a tree, in a curled leaf, a crevice, or some secluded nook in which to pupate; many go into the ground. Naked pupae—that is, pupae without a protective covering—do very well in their places of concealment and manage to survive.

In general the pupa has a shrunken, mummylike appearance (Figure 236) and, as a rule, is shorter in length than the larva. In most instances the mouth parts, antennae, legs, genital appendages, and wings appear as buds on the outside of the pupa. The wings and legs are functionless, and in cases where they are more than buds they may be appressed to the body, as with the pupae of moths. In the pupae of beetles the wings and legs are free, but enclosed in saclike cuticular sheaths. Usually the legs are not fully formed until near the end of the pupal stadium. The appendages in true flies are invisible, being obscured by the last larval skin.

If you gently squeeze a living pupa you will find that it will respond to your touch with a slight movement. This is usually the only response it will make. Most pupae are inactive, although there are exceptions such as the pupae of the mosquitoes and certain midges that are able to swim by moving the tail end of the body. Some pupae, like the aphis lion, become active and crawl about just before changing to the adult. Prior to the emergence of the adults, many pupae formed in wood, beneath bark, and in the ground free themselves from their resting places and make their way to the exterior. Some, like the pupae of the carpenter moths, have strong spines to help them work their way from cells in solid wood.

Sometimes when we spade our gardens we unearth a strange, brown, segmented, shell-like object having what appears to be a long handle at one end, as shown in Figure 247. This object is the pupa of the tomato horn-worm or tomato sphinx caterpillar. It is not unusual for pupae to take odd forms. The pupae of many of the sphinx moths as well

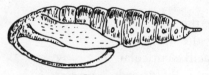

Figure 247
PUPA OF TOMATO HORNWORM

as the tomato sphinx are pitcherlike in outline. In these pupae the tongue is unusually
long, and is not appressed to the body but
is looped like the handle of a jug. Some naked
pupae resemble seeds (Figure 248). Others
are nymphlike. A few have conspicuous
cross-shaped jaws (Figure 249). The pupa of
the butterfly known as the wanderer resembles a spiral shell (Figure 250), although
when viewed from above, the anterior half
looks like a monkey's face (Figure 251). This

Figure 248
PUPARIUM OF HESSIAN FLY

one is really worth looking for. Or better still,
look for a colony of aphids on alder bushes
and other shrubs where you should find the
caterpillar. The caterpillar deviates far from
the usual habits of caterpillars, for it is carnivorous and feeds on plant lice. You will
probably find it buried beneath a mass of
aphids, covered with a web in which are
entangled fragments of its prey, frass, and
other materials. The caterpillar is easy to rear
if it is given plenty of aphids, and after a
while will change to the odd-shaped pupa.

Figure 249
CROSS-SHAPED JAWS OF PUPA
OF CADDIS FLY

Unlike other insects with a pupal stage, the
larvae of true flies pass the pupal stadium
within the last larval skin, which is not

broken until the adult flies are ready to emerge. The larval skin, which becomes hard and brown and which serves as a cocoon, is termed a puparium. In some species the puparium retains the form of the larva; in others the body of the larva shortens and assumes a more or less barrel-shaped form. The pupae of most flies escape from the puparium through a T-shaped opening on the back near the head (Figure 252); others through a crosswise split between the seventh and eighth abdominal segments. A few specialized flies have a bladderlike swelling on the head known as the ptilinum. This is inflated and pushed off. After the adult has emerged, the ptilinum is withdrawn into the head.

The transformation of a caterpillar to a butterfly, of a maggot to a fly, and a grub to a beetle involves some remarkable changes— changes that are necessary to fit the insect to a new environment or new food habits—that are not visible from the outside. Thus the prolegs of the caterpillar are lost and the mandibles are replaced with sucking mouth parts. The legless maggot becomes a six-legged fly. Wings are acquired in the majority of insects and reproductive organs are developed in all forms. In some species the gills of the larva are replaced by spiracles, the external openings of the respiratory system.

These are not the only changes that occur.

173

Figure 250
PUPA OF WANDERER

Figure 251
PUPA OF WANDERER

Figure 252
PUPARIUM OF A SOLDIER FLY

The old tissues forming the organs that are lost or replaced degenerate or break down, a process called histolysis. The disintegrating tissues and other debris are eaten and digested by cells called phagocytes. The substances produced by digestion then pass into the surrounding blood by diffusion and serve as nourishment for the new tissues that are built up after the old ones have been torn down. The process by which tissue is formed is called histogenesis. The extent to which all these changes take place varies greatly in different insects. In some species only a few organs are greatly modified; in others all the organs break down and are reformed, with certain exceptions like the central nervous system, the heart, and the reproductive system.

ADVENTURE 32

We Are Surprised to Learn of the Many Ways Insects Defend Themselves

MOST ANIMALS HAVE some sort of defense against their enemies, and insects are no exception. They have many ways of defending themselves—some, indeed, are quite unique —but in spite of the various protective devices the insects have developed, parasites and predaceous insects as well as other animals succeed in attacking and destroying them in vast numbers. These enemies, it must be remembered, also struggle for existence and must have food to survive. No protective device is foolproof, and though it may be ineffective against one kind of enemy, it is usually effective against another. A hairy caterpillar, for instance, may be eaten by one species of bird and left alone by others. This is better than to be eaten by all.

The chitinous exoskeleton of insects provides them with an armor that helps to ward off enemies. Some insects try to scare off enemies by noise. The May beetles (Figure 156) make a considerable racket that frequently frightens people and may also be instrumental in warding off an attack by an enemy, though we do not know whether this is so. The sand cricket (Figure 253), when attacked, faces its enemy and defies the aggressor by rubbing its hind legs vigorously against the sides of the abdomen, making a distinct rasping noise. When handled, many insects such as long-horned beetles and curculios make faint sounds, the cicada, a characteristic murmur when squeezed gently. The whirligig beetles, when disturbed, squeak by rubbing the tip of the abdomen against the elytra. Although these sounds are faint to the human ear, they may be exceedingly loud to other animals and cause these animals to drop the' insects.

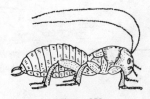

Figure 253
SAND CRICKET

Many insects, when disturbed or attacked, give off a defensive fluid. The "molasses" of the grasshopper is said to be ill-tasting and effective. A number of carabid beetles eject a pungent and often corrosive fluid from a pair

175

of anal glands. The fluid from the bombardier beetles volatilizes explosively on contact with the air (Figure 254). When one of these beetles is molested, it discharges the fluid which, on contact with the air, immediately turns into a fine spray that looks like smoke and at the same time gives off a distinct report reminding us of a miniature cannon. The performance is most interesting to watch. The insect can repeat the performance several times in rapid succession. The vapor is acid and corrosive and stains the human skin a rust-red color. Our American species is a small insect and is not harmful, but a South American relative that is considerably larger can burn and stain the flesh to such a degree that only a few of them can be taken with the naked hand.

In the Southwest and on the Pacific coast are beetles called pinacate bugs. When disturbed, these beetles defend themselves by elevating the hind end of the body and discharging, in the manner of the skunk, an oily fluid with a disagreeable odor.

The larva of the American sawfly (Figure 255) is able to squirt jets of a watery fluid from glands opening above the spiracles. Stinkbugs protect themselves by emitting a fluid with a disagreeable odor through two openings on the lower surface of the thorax behind or near the middle coxa. Similar glands occur in the bedbug on the upper surface of the first three abdominal segments. The larva of a certain leaf beetle is capable of emitting a liquid with a rather peculiar odor. Many insects have hypodermal glands that open into saclike invaginations of the body wall and that can be evaginated when the insects wish to make use of the secretions produced by these glands. Such organs are called osmeteria (Figure 256) (singular, osmeterium). Osmeteria are found in the larvae of our common swallowtail butterflies. They are forked, and when the caterpillars are disturbed they are thrust out from the upper part of the prothorax and give off a

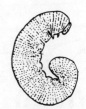

Figure 255
LARVA OF AMERICAN SAWFLY

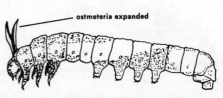

ostmeteria expanded

Figure 256
CATERPILLAR OF SWALLOWTAIL BUTTERFLY

characteristic but indescribable repellent odor. Find one of these caterpillars, squeeze it gently, and then with a hand lens observe what happens.

The larva of the puss moth has a rather curious spraying apparatus on the neck that discharges formic acid. Even the blood may serve as a repellent fluid. In ladybird beetles, fireflies, and oil beetles the blood contains cantharidine, an extremely caustic substance that is an almost perfect protection against birds, reptiles, and predaceous insects. In the oil beetles the blood issues as a yellow fluid from a pore at the end of the femur when the insects are handled. Our most common oil beetle is the buttercup oil beetle (Figure 257), found in meadows and pastures where it feeds on the leaves of various buttercups.

Hairs are probably more effective as a means of defense than odors or repellent fluids, since many birds will eat ill-flavored insects whereas they usually leave hairy caterpillars alone. Hairy caterpillars, like the fall webworm (Figure 258), the tent caterpillar (Figure 259), woolly bear (Figure 260), and

Figure 257
BUTTERCUP OIL BEETLE

Figure 258
CATERPILLAR OF FALL WEBWORM

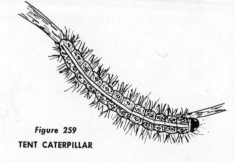

Figure 259
TENT CATERPILLAR

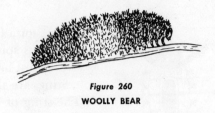

Figure 260
WOOLLY BEAR

gypsy moth are eaten by various birds, it is true, but such instances are exceptional. Hairs are also effective in protecting some hibernating caterpillars like the woolly bears from sudden changes in temperatures.

In many insects the hairs are also glandular and emit a malodorous, nauseous, or irritant fluid. Certain hairs on the caterpillars of the brown-tail moth secrete a fluid that produces an inflammation of the skin much like poison ivy. We should be very careful when picking up these caterpillars. The caterpillar of the io moth (Figure 261) should also be handled carefully, for it is armed with venomous spines. The spines are not only very sharp but brittle, and break easily. The saddleback caterpillar (Figure 262) and the spiny oak slug (Figure 263) also have venomous setae.

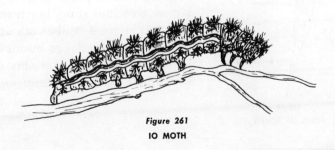

Figure 261
IO MOTH

Figure 262
SADDLEBACK CATERPILLAR

Figure 263
SPINY OAK SLUG

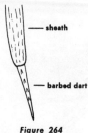

— sheath

— barbed dart

Figure 264
STING OF HONEY BEE

Except for a few cases like the cuckoos, these poisonous spines and hairs are highly defensive against birds.

Stings are also effective weapons of defense. The sting of the honeybee is a sharp, lance-like organ at the posterior part of the body. It is a complicated organ and consists of two barbed darts operated by strong muscles and enclosed in a sheath (Figure 264). Find a bee, dissect out the sting, and view it through a microscope. The darts are connected with a pair of glands that secrete the poison. One of the glands secretes an acid and the other an alkaline substance. It is believed that both fluids are necessary for a deadly effect and that in insects that simply paralyze their prey, like the solitary wasps, the alkaline glands are functionless. When a bee stings, the sting as well as the tip of the abdomen are torn from the insect's body as the barbs extend backward and catch in the flesh of the victim.

The white-faced hornet, the yellow jackets, and other wasps also have stings. The wasps use their stings primarily to paralyze caterpillars and spiders with which to provision their nests. The paper wasp is able to inflict a most ferocious sting, but is not easily provoked. The mud dauber can also sting, but usually goes about her business unless molested. Various species of ants are furnished with stings that inject formic acid into their victims. The fire ant, which has recently invaded our southern states, is extremely pugnacious and can inject a poison that causes a serious irritation.

Many insects use their jaws for defensive purposes. Ants, for instance, can inflict serious pain with their mandibles. The soldier members of the termite colony have enormous mandibles (Figure 265) that are used primarily for protective purposes, but there seems to be some question how effective they are.

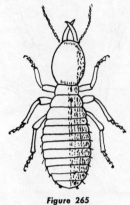

Figure 265
SOLDIER TERMITE

INSECTS NOT ONLY defend themselves against their enemies by aggressive means, like repellent glands, stings, spines, and other devices; they also do so in a passive way by resembling their surroundings and escaping detection. Our common walking stick, or stick insect (Figure 266) as it is more usually known, looks so much like a twig that it is often

ADVENTURE 33

We Learn of Some Ways Insects Escape Detection by Their Enemies

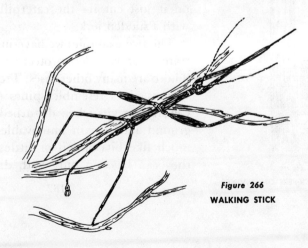

Figure 266
WALKING STICK

passed by. This curious insect is long and slender with long, thin legs that are well fitted for walking and may be either brown or green in color. Measuring worms also resemble the twigs on which they rest. These "worms" are the larvae of a group of moths and are also known as inchworms, spanworms, and loopers. When resting, they cling with their abdominal legs and stretch out their bodies straight, stiff, and motionless and look like twigs (Figure 267). You may wonder how a measuring worm can remain in such a position without becoming exhausted. There is no mystery about it. Look carefully and you will see that it has spun a strand of silk from the mouth and has attached the free end to its support. The thread serves as a guy rope, and if you think there is no tension on it just cut it—the caterpillar falls back with a sudden jerk.

The two examples we have just given illustrate what is called protective resemblance. There are many other cases. Tree hoppers on various vines resemble spines (Figure 268). Certain weevils when disturbed drop to the ground and remain immovable and look so much like bits of soil or little pebbles that they can be seen only with difficulty. The

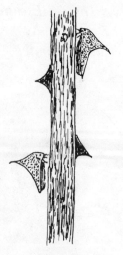

182

Figure 269
CATERPILLAR OF VICEROY BUTTERFLY

caterpillars of the viceroy butterfly (Figure 269) and the giant swallowtail, as well as other larvae, resemble the excrement of birds. In all these instances color adds to the protective disguise; the walking sticks are brown or green and the measuring worms are variously colored to blend with the twigs and leaves on which they feed.

Color is of distinct advantage to many insects, since they can escape detection by blending with their surroundings. This sort of camouflage is known as protective coloration. This is illustrated by the sawyer (Figure 270) and the catocala moth. These moths generally have brilliantly colored hind wings of red, orange, and black. Their front wings, however, vary in color from white to gray and brown. In flight they are readily seen, but when they alight or are at rest, the front wings cover the hind wings and the moths become inconspicuous; indeed, they look so much like the bark of a tree, on which they commonly rest, that they are barely discernible (Figure 271).

Figure 270
SAWYER

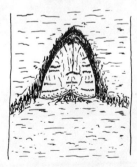

Figure 271
CATOCALA MOTH ON BIRCH

183

A number of insects have combined this folding of brilliant wings with a cessation of motion. The bella moth, for instance, has hind wings that are conspicuously red with black markings and front wings that are cream-colored and less conspicuous. This moth has the habit of dropping suddenly into the grass and folding its wings; to follow it to its resting place is almost impossible. Tiger beetles and grasshoppers have a similar habit of coming to an abrupt halt. The next time you frighten a tiger beetle or a Carolina locust into flight, note how it suddenly drops to the ground and then takes a step or two to one side to make it even more difficult to find it.

Many grasshoppers have showy wings that are obscured by the wing covers when the insects are at rest. Most of us have noticed how much grasshoppers resemble the soil in color. The Carolina locust, which is often seen on roadsides, waste places, and on well-beaten paths, may barely be distinguished against the ground. Study the grasshoppers and you will find that they not only vary greatly in color, ranging from ashy gray to yellowish or to reddish brown, but that they are usually found on soil their own color. If you live near the Atlantic coast you might look for the seaside locust. You may have some difficulty finding it, for it is practically invisible against the gray sand of the seashore and the chances are you won't see it unless it is disturbed into flight. The same species also occurs along the shores of inland lakes, where it is pale brown to match the brown sands on which it lives. A related species is found only on rock surfaces, either bare or lichen-crusted. The insect is mottled with several colors, yellow, black, and greenish, and is quite noticeable when flying. When at rest on a rock or a patch of lichens, it can barely be seen. It is interesting to observe that in an area of lichen-covered rocks the insect habitually flies from one patch of lichens to another; rarely does it alight on the ground.

A great many caterpillars are protectively colored by the leaves on which they feed. The larva of Harris's sphinx (Figure 111) feeds in a group of pine needles and is well concealed, since the body is marked with longitudinal green-and-white stripes that simulate a bunch of pine needles. Numerous grass-eating caterpillars are striped with green and the large green sphinx caterpillars, despite their size, are not readily seen because of their oblique lateral stripes that divide a solid mass of green, like that of a leaf, into smaller sections (Figure 272). The unicorn caterpillar, which is green with brown patches, rests

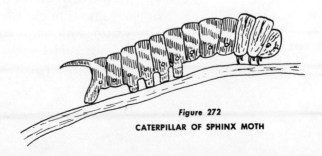

Figure 272
CATERPILLAR OF SPHINX MOTH

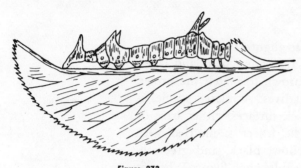

Figure 273
UNICORN CATERPILLAR
ON BASSWOOD LEAF

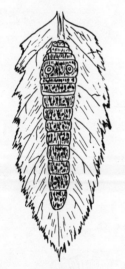

Figure 274
CATERPILLAR OF TIGER SWALLOWTAIL

for hours along the eaten or torn edge of a basswood leaf and in this position has a deceptive resemblance to the partially dead border of the leaf (Figure 273).

In contrast to the insects that are protectively colored, there are many that have hideous colors or markings or are so vividly colored as to be quite conspicuous. The caterpillar of the tiger swallowtail has two large greenish yellow spots, edged with black and enclosing small black spots, on the sides of the thorax (Figure 274). The eyed elater has two large black velvety eyelike spots on the prothorax (Figure 275). In both cases the spots are presumed to frighten enemies. Some of the spots and markings on the wings of butterflies are believed to direct the birds away from the vital parts of the insect's body.

In many insects bright colors or markings are associated with such various defensive devices as stings, spines, odors, repellent fluids

186

and the like. As such insects are unpalatable
or otherwise undesirable, the colors are of
advantage if they exempt their owners from
attack. The brightly colored harlequin cabbage bug (Figure 276) is usually left alone by
birds. So, too, are the ill-flavored lady beetles
and various leaf beetles like the elm leaf
beetle. The rose chafer, the soldier beetle,
and the locust borer are also avoided. They
are, however, exceptional cases. The fact is
that warning colors are effective against some
enemies, ineffective against others.

Many insects imitate an obnoxious or distasteful species and are therefore left alone.
The protection may take the form of stings,
hairs, bristles, unpleasant odors, or other protective devices. A familiar example of this
protective mimicry, as it is called, is af-
forded by two common species of butterflies:
the monarch and viceroy. The monarch is
the familiar large butterfly with reddish
brown wings marked with black veins and
white spots along the edges that we see so
often flying about during the summer. It is
also known as the milkweed butterfly, since
the caterpillars feed on milkweed. This butterfly is said to be unpalatable and distasteful
to birds and is accordingly left alone. The
viceroy butterfly, which is presumed to be
"good eating," resembles the monarch, although somewhat smaller, and is also left
alone, the assumption being that birds can-

Figure 275
EYED ELATER

Figure 276
HARLEQUIN CABBAGE BUG

187

Figure 277
DRONE FLY

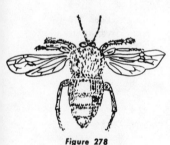

Figure 278
DRONE HONEYBEE

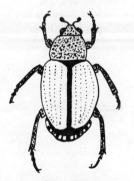

Figure 279
JAPANESE BEETLE

not detect any difference between the two. There is no evidence, however, that the viceroy profits by this resemblance, although it may have done so at one time.

The common drone fly (Figure 277) mimics the honeybee (Figure 278) in form, size, and coloration and the manner in which it buzzes around flowers. You have probably often seen it and mistaken it for the bee. It does not fool the kingbird and flicker, however. A familiar species of flower fly mimics the yellow jacket; indeed, flower flies are good imitators, for another species looks much like the bumblebee. So, too, do certain robber flies. Quite a few insects mimic ants.

A large number of larvae and pupae probably mimic one another, but since little work has been done in regard to these relationships, we know little about them. Probably the chief reason they have been neglected is that the larvae and pupae are not generally highly colored and fail to attract attention. Consider, for instance, the caterpillar of the pipe-vine swallowtail and the caterpillar of the mourning cloak. They are both dark-colored, are furnished with spinelike protuberances, and have conspicuous yellow or reddish spots. The pipe-vine caterpillar has a gland that emits a disagreeable odor. The caterpillar of the mourning cloak does not have such a gland. Does it share the protection given the swallowtail caterpillar? This

188

and other possible imitations offer an interesting field for investigation.

MANY INSECTS LIVE in the ground. Most of them spend only a short time below the surface—a few days perhaps—as eggs, larvae, or pupae. Others remain for longer periods. The Japanese beetle (Figure 279) spends almost eleven months of the year in the ground as egg, larva, and pupa. It emerges as an adult to feed and mate and then returns to the soil to lay its eggs. White grubs (Figure 280), the larvae of the May beetles, spend two to three years in the soil; wireworms (Figure 281), the larvae of the click beetles, from two to six years. As a nymph, the periodical cicada remains in the ground for sixteen years in the north and for thirteen years in the south. The mole cricket and sand cricket (Figure 253) live most of their lives in the soil, mating and laying their eggs there, and certain ground beetles live continually in small pockets in the soil and never come to the surface. However long they stay there, whether it is throughout their entire existence or only a short part of it, they are all known as subterranean insects.

Few insects live in the soil as adults. In addition to the mole and sand crickets and the ground beetles there are the small shore bugs, the toad bugs (Figure 282), ants, ter-

189

We Discuss the Insects That Live in the Ground

Figure 280
WHITE GRUB

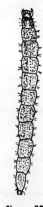

Figure 281
WIREWORM

mites, and certain wasps and bees. Nymphs, too, are commonly absent in the soil, though certain root-feeding aphids may be found there. The cicada, of course, is the classic example. A few naiads of the dragonflies and mayflies burrow in the mud. But for the most part insects that live in the soil do so as eggs, larvae, and pupae.

Why do insects seek the soil or live a subterranean existence if only for a short time? There are three reasons: to obtain food, to store food, and for protection. Eggs laid in the soil are protected from drying and to some degree from predators and parasites. The larvae of the Japanese beetle feed on the roots of living plants. So, too, do the white grubs. The wireworms feed on seeds and roots; the larvae of the green June beetle upon vegetable mold; the larvae of the oriental beetle on decayed sod; and the tumble beetles, dung beetles, and earth-boring beetles upon excrement.

Various species store food beneath the surface of the ground. Ants store nectar, pollen, seeds, parts of plants, and other material in their nests. Certain wasps that make burrows for their young provision them with caterpillars and spiders. The cicada killer places cicadas in her nest.

The depth to which insects penetrate the soil varies with different species. The type of the soil and the season of the year are also factors. Some of the ground beetles go beneath the surface for only a fraction of an inch. Generally speaking, insects may be found within four inches of the surface during the summer, but when winter comes they penetrate deeper. The cicada is said to descend to a depth of eighteen feet. Some species excavate burrows that may extend quite some distance into the ground. The cicada killer has been known to dig its burrow thirteen inches beneath the surface, but this is a short distance compared to the burrows of some of the tiger beetles that may extend down as far as seventy-two inches.

Like most other insects, the subterranean forms have their problems. One is moisture, which at times can become so excessive, the insects drown. An undue amount of moisture is also conducive to the growth of fungi and bacteria; wireworms and white grubs are especially susceptible to attacks by these plants. Sometimes the lack of moisture has disastrous results. To prevent undue evaporation of soil moisture, certain tiger beetles plug the openings of their burrows when the soil becomes dry.

A subterranean habit may enable various insects to escape predatory and parasitic species, but such a habit often introduces another unfriendly element in the form of moles and mice. Some of the burrowing wasps build turrets over entrances that protect them while at work. Other ground-in-habiting insects like the burrowing bees stand guard at the entrance to their nest, filling the opening with their heads. One of the chief problems is how to dispose of excavated material. Ants deposit the excavated particles of soil around the entrance to their nests, forming the characteristic mounds. Certain wasps do the same thing, while others scatter the excavated material about the entrance. Tiger beetles carry the excavated soil a considerable distance from their burrows so the particles of soil will not interfere with the proper functioning of the burrow, which is essentially a trap. If the soil particles were deposited about the entrance, the piles or mounds would likely divert any approaching insect from the burrow. The wireworms and white grubs employ a rather simple means of getting rid of excavated material: they simply compress it against the walls of their burrows.

ADVENTURE 35

We Inspect Some Subterranean Dwellings

ANTS ARE, PERHAPS, the most familiar of the insects and we all know that some of them live in underground nests that they excavate in the soil. The excavated material is brought to the surface and deposited in mounds or craters around the entrance—the familiar anthills. Few of us, however, are aware that

192

the mounds differ and may be a clue to the species that occupy the subterranean nests.

An ant nest may be, and often is, a complex labyrinth of subterranean galleries and frequently consists of long underground passageways that extend in all directions. Unlike the social bees and wasps, the ants do not construct permanent brood cells but place their young in chambers. After a rain ants make every effort to improve the nest by pressing the earth into the walls of the galleries, using a fluid they secrete as a cement. Sometimes they incorporate sticks and stones in the walls.

Some ants excavate their nests in the open; others under a stone (Figure 283) or sheltering herbage. The reason for building beneath a stone is that the sun warms the stone, which in turn radiates heat into the underground galleries. Much the same effect is accomplished by excavating under herbage or by making a mound with a hard cemented roof. The mounds may be small and consist simply of excavated particles, as that of the cornfield ant (Figure 284), or they may by huge, as

Figure 283

ANT NEST BENEATH A STONE

Figure 284
MOUND OF CORNFIELD ANT

much as three or four feet in diameter and a foot or two high and contain labyrinthine passages in addition to those underground. The mounds of the mound-building ant are elaborate structures frequently covered with twigs, dead leaves, grass, and all kinds of foreign materials, and may last almost indefinitely.

Although most of the insects that live in the ground do so for only a comparatively short time, many of them excavate well-defined tunnels or burrows as temporary shelters. To some of us an insect burrow may be only a hole in the ground and one burrow, at a casual glance, may look much like another, but if we examine a few of them we find they reveal characteristic differences that identify them much as the leaf mines, the galleries and tunnels of the wood borers, and the galls characterize their makers. Direction, diameter, length and type, whether open or closed, and simple or branched are some of the features that distinguish the burrows. Other features are habitat or location in regard to the kind of soil, whether clay, sand, or loam; the condition of the soil, whether loose or compact; the size of the particles excavated; the weight, structure, and type of soil excavated; the nature of the interior; and the quantity and kind of materials stored in the burrows.

Let us consider the burrows of the tiger beetles. The larvae usually construct tunnels perpendicular to the surface of the ground, although a few species build in the sides of banks. The burrows measure about two tenths of an inch in diameter and extend downward from twelve to fifteen inches (Figure 285). They are generally excavated in clay or sand and are unbranched. Although the larvae use their heads to close them, they are considered to be open. Some tiger beetles, for instance a species found in Kansas and other western states, are gregarious. Two to twelve grubs may dig burrows within a radius of ten inches.

In contrast to these vertical burrows of the tiger beetles, the larvae of some of the ground beetles construct horizontal burrows on the surface of the ground (Figure 286). They are usually excavated in soils rich with humus, are very small in diameter, and extend from three to ten inches in length. They are unbranched and open. Unlike its relatives, *Harpalus*, one of the largest ground beetles, digs in loam a simple, curved burrow six to seven inches long (Figure 287). It also builds a distinct mound over the entrance. Another species, *Geopinus*, excavates a burrow at an

Figure 285
BURROW OF TIGER BEETLE

Figure 286
SURFACE BURROW
OF GROUND WASP

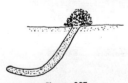

Figure 287
BURROW OF *HARPALUS*

195

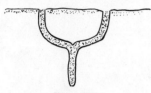

angle of forty-five degrees in a sand dune. It is a short burrow, running only three to four inches, and is unbranched. It also has a mound at the entrance.

The burrows of many subterranean insects are then not merely holes in the ground, but well-defined tunnels with their own specific characteristics. The tumblebugs, June beetles, and click beetles all excavate unbranched tunnels, but the tumblebugs dig a vertical one in sand, the June beetles a horizontal one in dry loam, and the click beetles a winding one in moist loam. A scarabid beetle builds a burrow with two entrances (Figure 288). The entrances extend downward for a short distance and then join to form a vertical burrow that may be as much as ten inches deep.

The burrows of the burrowing wasps, which are actually nests for the young, show considerable variations. A bembecine wasp excavates an unbranched tunnel at an angle of forty-five degrees (Figure 289); a eumenid wasp, a vertical burrow that may be either branched or unbranched. Both of these insects build in compact soil and both close their burrows. Some eumenid wasps construct turrets (Figure 290) while the burrows are in process of being constructed which are removed when the nests are completed, the material being used to close the openings. The cicada killer builds a turret only when the nest is completed.

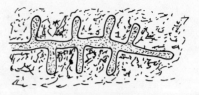

Figure 291
BURROW OF HALICTUS

Bees that burrow in the ground are known as mining bees. Some of them excavate in level ground; others dig tunnels in the vertical sides of banks. They are, as a rule, gregarious, and as many as one hundred burrows have been found in a small area in a claybank.

If we examine the burrows—or nests, for that is what they are—of *Halictus* in midsummer, we find them to be a tunnel extending into the bank and from it smaller, short tunnels, each leading to a cell (Figure 291). The cells are lined with a thin coating of firm clay and may be open or closed. The closed cells contain either a mass of pollen and nectar with an egg upon it or a larva feeding on the food stored for it.

An interesting feature of these nests is that several bees use the main tunnel as a corridor or passageway to the cells they are building and provisioning, but the corridor is not a public one. It is constricted at the outer end and is guarded by a sentinel whose head nearly fills the opening (Figure 292). When a bee arrives at the entrance the sentinel backs

Figure 292
SENTINEL GUARDING ENTRANCE
TO NEST

into the wider part of the corridor and allows the other to enter, if it has the right of access, and then immediately resumes its position as a guard. But if the bee is a stranger the sentinel remains immovable and refuses admittance.

The nests of *Anthophora* are excavated in steeply inclined or perpendicular banks of earth, preferably in those of compact clay. The tunnel extends into the bank a variable distance and leads to a cluster of oval cells. The layer of earth forming a wall of a cell is made firm by a cementing substance. The waterproofing of the wall of the cell is an essential feature, for without it the semifluid mass of pollen and nectar with which the cell is provisioned would be partially absorbed by the wall of the cell.

The entrance to these tunnels is provided with a cylindrical tube of clay extending outward and downward (Figure 293). The tube is rough on the outside but smooth within.

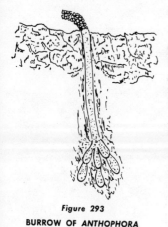

Figure 293
BURROW OF ANTHOPHORA

198

It is composed of small pellets of earth. These pellets, when brought from the tunnel, are wet and easily molded into the desired form, but soon become dry and firm. How can the wetness of these pellets be explained? When nest-building, the bees go to a place where water is available and after lapping up a supply, fly to the nest, where the water is used to soften the clay.

The nests of *Andrena* are vertical tunnels in roadsides and in fields of scanty vegetation. The burrows have broad cells branching from them (Figure 294). Each female builds her own nest, but frequently the females build their nests near one another, forming large villages.

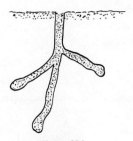

Figure 294
BURROW OF ANDRENA

It is interesting to note that some of these burrowing insects select open places void of grass and other herbage, while others go to some lengths to conceal them. The bembecine wasps, for instance, select open places but some eumenid wasps conceal the opening of their nests in a clump of grass or beneath a small stone.

ALTHOUGH THE VAST MAJORITY of insects simply lay their eggs and then completely forget about them, leaving their young to find their own food, many provide food either by feeding their young day by day, like ants, honeybees, and other social insects, or, like

ADVENTURE 36

We Discover a New Meaning for the Word "Solitary"

the mud dauber and carpenter bee, by storing food for their young so that when they hatch they have a supply right on hand.

On the basis of food supply we can conveniently group insects into three classes: the non-solitary or non-social, the solitary,* and the social. In the first class belong the insects that do not provide food for their young; in the second class belong the insects that store food for their young (a method of feeding called mass provisioning); and in the third class belong the insects that feed their young each day (called progressive provisioning). Several other characteristics distinguish these three classes. For instance, the free feeders (or non-solitary or non-social insects) do not construct a nest, but both the solitary and social forms do. No caste system or division of labor such as exists in the social insects occurs in either the free feeders or solitary insects, nor is parental care, which is typical of the social insects, exercised by either the free feeders or the solitary forms. There are many insects whose habits approximate those of these three classes; hence they are somewhat difficult to classify. Certain tumble beetles are regarded by some entomologists as social insects because the adults guard the eggs until they hatch, but since they practice mass provisioning and lack many of the characteristics of the social insects, they are more

* Some entomologists prefer the word subsocial.

like the solitary forms. Then there are certain wasps that feed their young from day to day. As these insects represent indeterminate forms, it is apparent that the three groups intergrade with one another and that no sharp or distinct line can be drawn between them.

The solitary insects are, for the most part, bees and wasps. Most of them excavate burrows in the ground for nests; some tunnel in the pith of plants and then divide the tunnel into cells by building partitions across the tunnels; and a few build nests of mud or vegetable material which they fasten to the trunks of trees, rocks, or other surfaces. Those that build such nests are usually wasps, and if one of them will cooperate you can observe at close quarters how it builds its nest and later the activities of the developing young. Get a spool, cut it lengthwise a little off center, leaving as much of the hole as you can, cover the exposed side with a piece of cellophane to provide a window through which you can watch what goes on in the nest, and then fasten the spool securely to a sill outside a window (Figure 295). The rest is a matter of luck.

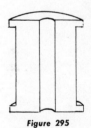

Figure 295
CUT SPOOL TO PROVIDE
NESTING SITE FOR WASP

The solitary bees provision their nests with pollen and nectar. Some wasps use the same material but most of them use animal matter like caterpillars and spiders. The spider hunters capture and paralyze a single large

201

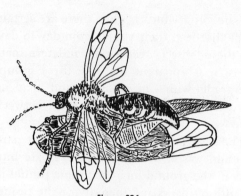

Figure 296
CICADA KILLER CARRYING CICADA
TO BURROW

spider, which provides enough food for one wasp larva, but the mud daubers use small spiders, as many as twenty or more to a single cell. Other wasps use various insects like grasshoppers, cutworms, ants, bees, beetles, and other kinds. The cicada killer provisions her nest only with cicadas (Figure 296).

A few beetles can also be classified as solitary. The earth-boring beetles burrow into the ground or beneath dung, or they lay an egg on a mass of dung which serves as food for the young. The curculionids make compact rolls from leaves of the trees on which they feed and lay an egg in each roll. In neither case do the females give the young any further attention.

MOST OF US are familiar with the complex communities of honeybees and ants, since much has been written about them. These insects, like yellow jackets, paper wasps, termites, and bumblebees, live together in organized groups or colonies, in which there is a division of labor. For this reason they are known as social insects.

Social insects have a number of characteristics in common, such as provisioning, parental care, which involves the day-to-day feeding of the young, and division of labor. They all construct more or less elaborate nests and frequently build up large populations. Colonies of some tropical species of termites may consist of several million members. The communities of our social insects do not reach such proportions. The paper wasp, *Polistes,* may have a colony of only fifty individuals, and a populous colony of bumblebees may consist of three to four hundred members. The communities of the bald-faced hornet and the honeybee are, however, much larger; that of the wasp may have as many as fifteen thousand individuals, that of the honeybee anywhere from thirty-five to fifty thousand. Obviously in an organized community of this sort there has to be cooperation and division of labor, but we must point out that the insects do not cooperate intentionally; they do so as a natural sequence of division of labor. Nor does the queen, as the

ADVENTURE 37

We Pay a Call on the Social Insects

203

term may imply, rule the colony. The social insects do not solve their problems by any executive decree, judicial ruling, or legislative act; they do not, as a matter of fact, have such bodies.

The colonies of the paper wasps and bumblebees are temporary and endure for only a year. As cold weather arrives, all the members of a colony die except the queen. She passes the winter in a secluded retreat and the following spring establishes a new colony. The ants, termites, honeybees, and the stingless bees of the tropics maintain permanent or perennial colonies. However, they establish new colonies when the sexes leave the nest on their nuptial flight or when conditions become too congested, which occurs often in the hive of the honeybee. Then the old queen leaves the hive, accompanied by most of the workers, and founds a new colony, a phenomenon known as swarming.

Perhaps the most outstanding feature of the social insects is their caste system. By definition a caste is basically a division or class of society in a community, but in entomology it is one of the polymorphic forms of the social insects, each form or caste having its particular share in the duties and work of perpetuating the colony (division of labor). There are generally three castes: the females or queens, the workers, and the males. The queen's primary function is to lay eggs, and as a rule there is only one mature queen in a colony at one time, although new queens may be developed for emergencies or to lead forth new colonies at the time of swarming. The duties of the workers include all the functions necessary for the maintenance and perpetuation of the colony, such as taking care of and feeding the young as well as the queen, gathering and storing food, repairing the nest and adding on more sections, and keeping it clean. The males' only duty is to mate with the queen.

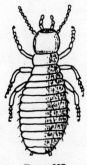

Figure 297
WORKER TERMITE

Termites—somewhat surprisingly, since they are not as high on the scale of insect evolution as ants and bees—have a most highly developed caste system. In most species there are four castes, each of which, unlike the castes of the other social insects, includes both male and female individuals. These four castes consist of the workers (Figure 297), which are the most numerous and which carry on all the domestic duties of the colony; fertile males and females with fully developed wings (Figure 298); fertile males and females with undeveloped wings; and the soldiers

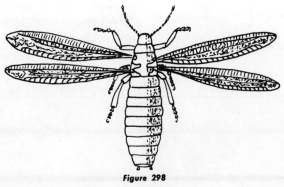

Figure 298
MALE TERMITE

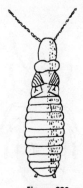

Figure 299
MALE TERMITE WITH
UNDEVELOPED WINGS

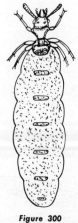

Figure 300
TERMITE QUEEN

(Figure 299). The sexually mature males and females with fully developed wings are the ones that fly forth from the nest, mate, and establish a new colony. After the nuptial flight the mating pair, known as the king and queen, burrow into a crevice and shed their wings, leaving four triangular stumps (Figure 299). They establish a new colony and once the colony is under way, they live sheltered in a special chamber.

The queen meanwhile becomes enormously distended with eggs and is incapable of locomotion (Figure 300). She can lay an astonishing number of eggs—in the thousands, sometimes as many as sixty per minute. The males and females with undeveloped wings are forms held in reserve in case something should happen to the "reigning" royal pair. We use the word "reigning" somewhat advisedly because neither the king nor queen controls or influences the activities of the colony; their only function is to provide off-spring. The fourth caste, or soldiers, are like the workers and are of either sex with undeveloped sexual organs but with monstrous mandibles and heads. Their chief duty is to protect the colony, although they sometimes fail to do so. Whenever you find a stump or log or a decayed fence post, break it open. You may find it inhabited by termites, which are most interesting to examine with a hand lens.

All the members of colonies of honeybees and stingless bees are winged, but worker ants are wingless and in some species the females also. Among the ants polymorphism is common. In other words a single species may occur in a variety of forms. In some species there may be several types of workers that are distinguished by structural peculiarities of one kind or another. All three castes may have large forms or dwarf forms, the workers being called workers major and workers minor. The sexual individuals are not necessarily winged. Some or all of them, especially the females, may resemble the workers in having no wings and for this reason are called ergatoid. You might dig up an ant colony here and there and look for these various forms. They will repay you for your effort.

With the exception of the stingless bees of the tropics that practice mass provisioning, social insects feed the larvae from day to day. Since the larvae require considerable attention for a fairly long time, only a few can be raised by a single female. In a large colony where a number of young are reared at the same time, an army of workers is needed. The food fed to the young varies according to the species. Newly hatched termites, for instance, receive only saliva but later are fed regurgitated food and finally wood, the staple food of termites. The young of the bald-faced hornet are fed at first on regurgitated food consisting of nectar and fruit juices, later on masticated insects. Nectar and pollen are given to the larvae of bumblebees and honeybees. The larvae of ants are fed a variety of food according to the species. Their diet includes nectar, sap, honeydew, fruit juices, leaves, fungi, and other plant material.

In addition to being fed, the young of social insects are also kept clean by the workers, who also remove dead insects and other debris from the nest. The workers take special care of the queens. In both ant and termite colonies the queens are not only fed and kept clean, but their eggs are carried away and placed in the proper chamber. In summer the workers of the beehive cool the hive by fanning their wings and in winter protect the queen from low temperatures by clustering about her. In an ant colony the workers are always on the alert to take advantage of changes in temperature and moisture. It is a common practice for ants to feed one another from mouth to mouth. On their return to the nest the workers who have been out foraging feed those who remained at home, and these in return offer regurgitated food to the foragers. Frequently an exchange of food may occur between the young and the adults. The young of both the ants and termites eject a substance relished by the workers. The young of the paper wasps have similar habits. This exchange of food is not necessarily confined to members of the same species, but may take place between insects of different species. Certain ants, for instance, not only tolerate the presence of rove beetles but treat them like members of the colony simply because the beetles secrete a fluid desired by the ants. The exchange of food, known as trophallaxis —which, incidentally, has not been observed among the social bees—is considered by some entomologists as the source of the social habit in wasps, ants, and termites.

ADVENTURE 38

We Visit Some Homes of Wax

IN EARLY SPRING we often see bumblebees, in their rich, velvety costumes of black and gold, with their wings yet untorn from long foraging flights, humming their way over fields and meadows (Figure 301). These bees are the queens and the only survivors of last year's colonies. Their mission in life is to establish new colonies, but instead of getting to work immediately they fly about for a week or so,

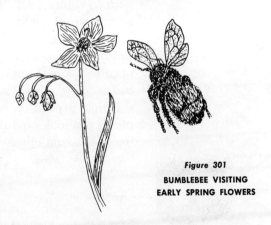

Figure 301
BUMBLEBEE VISITING
EARLY SPRING FLOWERS

sipping the nectar of early spring flowers and filling the baskets on their hind legs with pollen grains. This activity is not without purpose, for after a fast of eight or nine months they must store up energy in preparation for their domestic duties and obtain the food necessary to feed the growing grubs of the new colony.

The queen usually selects the abandoned nest of a field mouse or chipmunk, although it may be merely a depression in a field in which to build her nest. Having selected her site, she gathers the softest and finest material she can find into a heap and in the center excavates a cavity with an entrance at one side just large enough for her to pass in and out. She next makes a lump of pollen and honey in the center of the floor of the cavity and on top of the lump, using her jaws to do so, fashions a circular wall of wax to form a cell. Inside it she lays her eggs and seals the cell with wax. Then she constructs a waxen pot in the entrance to the nest and fills it with honey (Figure 302). This honey serves as a reserve supply of food, for the queen sits on her eggs like an incubating hen to keep them warm. On pleasant days she may venture out to collect honey, but during the night and in bad weather when food cannot be obtained she must depend on her stored-up food supply. If you look carefully in the spring before the grasses and other vegetation becomes too

210

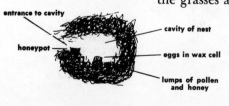

entrance to cavity

cavity of nest

honeypot

eggs in wax cell

lumps of pollen and honey

Figure 302
BUMBLEBEE NEST IN SPRING

high, you may find one of these nests and see for yourself how it is made.

The nest or comb of the honeybee is quite an elaborate structure compared to the nest of the bumblebee. The wild bees build their wax combs in a hollow tree; the domesticated species, in a hive provided for the purpose. The wax the insects use is secreted by four pairs of wax glands located on the ventral wall of the second, third, fourth, and fifth abdominal segments of the worker bees. Each gland is simply a disclike area of the hypodermis. The cuticle covering each gland is smooth and delicate and is known as a wax plate. The wax is exuded through these plates and accumulates, forming little scales that are used in making honeycomb.

The comb is not built by an individual bee, but by the collected efforts of many. When a comb is to be constructed, the workers gather together in a curtainlike mass and cling to one another by their feet, each bee taking hold by its forefeet of the hind feet of the one above it, the uppermost bees clinging to some support in the hive or the hollow of the tree. Heat is generated by this mass and after a while white films of wax appear under the abdomen. These films of wax are transferred to the mouth, where they are mixed with a fluid from the cephalic glands that changes the chemical composition of the wax and makes it plastic.

211

Figure 303
BASES OF COMB CELLS

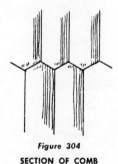

Figure 304
SECTION OF COMB

When the wax has been made the right consistency, the bees use it to construct a vertical hanging wall, or septum. Once the wall has been built, the bees bite out pits on opposite sides. These pits are the bottoms of the future cells, the excavated wax being used to make the cell walls. The bottom of each cell consists of three rhombic plates (Figure 303) and the cells of one side interlock with those of the other in such a way that each rhombic serves for two cells (Figure 304). As the wax is a precious substance, the bees use it with the greatest economy; hence they scrape the walls to paper thinness.

The cells are more or less hexagonal (Figure 305) in shape, but by no means hexagonal in the mathematical sense, for it is difficult to find a cell with errors of less than three or four degrees in the angles. Worker cells are one fifth of an inch in diameter, while the large cells destined for the drones or for the storage of honey are one quarter of an inch across (Figure 306). The honey is retained in the cell by a cap of wax. It consists of a cir-

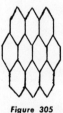

Figure 305
WORKER CELLS

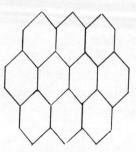

Figure 306
DRONE CELLS

cular disc at the middle supported from the angles of the cell by six tiny girders. The cells occupied by the queens are unlike the hexagonal cells of the hive. They are considerably larger, cylindrical, and vertical (Figure 307). To strengthen the edges of the cells, to fill crevices, or to make repairs, the workers use a sticky exudation called propolis, obtained from the buds or leaf axils of various trees, although they will at times use artificial substances like grease, pitch, or varnish. With the approach of winter, propolis is used liberally by the bees to make their abode tight and comfortable.

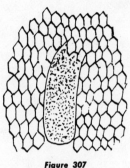

Figure 307
QUEEN CELLS

As WE WATCH the mud dauber at work building her nest, it does not occur to us that mud daubers have been building the same kind of nest for thousands of years, perhaps ever since they appeared on earth, and that each mud dauber builds a nest identical with the one from which it came and identical with those of other mud daubers. Once having completed her nest, she provisions it with the correct kind of food and lays her eggs in it in the proper manner. She does all this without previous experience or instruction. We call it instinct.

But what is instinct? No one yet has been able to define the word satisfactorily. It is a vague sort of word and susceptible to various

ADVENTURE 39

We Analyze
Insect Behavior

meanings. We might say that an instinct is the response or reaction of an organism to one or more stimuli. A stimulus evokes a certain response known as a tropism. The response is involuntary and is simply a reflex act. Hence a series of instinctive actions must consist of a number of coordinated reflexes; in short, complex chains of tropisms. Put differently, a complex instinctive action is a chain, each link being a simple reflex act. We must not presume that all stimuli are external like light, heat, etc.; they can also be internal. Moreover instincts cannot be inherited; what can be inherited is the ability to respond in a specific way to various stimuli.

Perhaps we can explain instinct by saying that it is carried out without previous knowledge, experience, or training; it is usually a series of reflex acts in response to chemical and physical stimuli; it generally proceeds in a regular sequence; and, as a rule, it is inflexible though it can be modified.

Let us see how all this applies to the mud dauber. The insect certainly has no training or instruction as to the type of nest to build, the kind of materials to use, or in the selections of a site. The construction of the nest, followed by the stinging of the prey, carrying the prey to the nest, and laying the eggs on it is merely a series of reflex acts in response to various stimuli—an internal urge to lay eggs, the selection of the right kind of mud probably determined by the stimuli of touch and taste, and the capture of prey also probably through the stimuli of sight and smell. Moreover operations are carried out in the proper sequence, this sequence of events being called the rhythm of instinct.

This rhythm of instinct, which is generally inflexible, is well illustrated by the potter wasp. The nesting habits of this insect are carried out in four distinct steps: building the nest; provisioning it with caterpillars; suspending an egg from the ceiling of the nest; and sealing the nest. If, at the time the wasp is engaged in provisioning her nest, a small hole is cut in it, the wasp will not interrupt her labors to mend or repair the nest but will continue to provision it, then lay her egg and close the nest. If, however, a hole is cut in the rim of the nest at the time she is finishing it, she will stop and repair it. In other words, the wasp cannot be deterred from following her sequence of operations but will continue inflexibly her series of operations to the end, though that end may not be entirely successful, as in this instance when she completed her nest with a hole in its side.

What this shows is that the stimuli that evoke instincts must be strong and that they proceed in a regular sequence. If an insect is interrupted in any stage, it cannot go back and perform an act that does not fall in the sequence. If interrupted, it can do one of two things: go back to the beginning and start all over again, or continue with subsequent steps, even though doing so many result in all operations' being futile. What it cannot do is to go back a step or two and do something not in the natural sequence. Moreover if an insect is prevented from carrying out an act it is accustomed to perform, it is completely at a loss how to proceed. Thus if a wasp habitually carries a grasshopper to its nest with its antennae, it will be unable to transport it if the antennae are cut off. Similarly if a caterpillar accustomed to feeding on a certain kind of food plant is transferred to another kind, it will starve rather than adopt the new food plant.

However, instincts are not completely inflexible and insects can and often do modify their habits. If you have a keen eye for observations you can detect variations in the performance of any instinctive act, variations that might be considered analogous to variations in structure. A mud dauber, for instance, may attach its nest to a new kind of support if necessary and may show slight variations in its normal type of architecture. The mud is usually smoothed over the exterior of the nest, but occasionally a wasp will leave pellets of mud clinging to the exterior. Sometimes a wasp will make use of an old nest instead of building a new one. A

216

wasp that normally uses its head to pound down the earth about the entrance to its nest has been observed using a small stone instead. A caterpillar will normally not adjust to a new food plant but if fed the leaves of a new food plant upon hatching, will feed on them. Among caterpillars that have exhausted their normal food supply, a few will sometimes adopt a new food plant and survive although the rest of their companions will refuse to do so, and starve. Frequently instinct may become blended with experience and modified as a result. The first flights of a dragonfly are purely instinctive and erratic; later, through experience, its flights become more controlled. However, when once shaped by experience, instinctive actions tend to become strong habits, and an act become so strengthened through repetition that any other course becomes impossible.

That instinctive responses are initiated by stimuli appears to be the only way we can explain insect behavior. The first movement of a caterpillar within the egg is doubtless due to some sensation, a sensation being merely the result of a stimulus, probably of temperature. Next, contact with the egg shell sets the jaws into action and the caterpillar eats its way out of the shell, though it has no way of knowing that by doing so it will escape from the shell. As it feeds, it cannot be aware that it is storing up food against the time when it changes

217

into a winged adult. When that time comes, it constructs a shelter similar to that built by other caterpillars that have emerged from the same batch of eggs. A butterfly, presumably through a sense of smell or some other stimulus, selects a specific plant on which to lay her eggs; otherwise how can we explain the monarch's selection of the milkweed or closely related species? To say that she "knows" the milkweed and that only the milkweed will serve her purpose is to give her a certain amount of intelligence or imply a degree of reasoning power, when the fact of the matter is that egg laying is not performed until evoked by some kind of stimulus, in this particular case probably an olfactory one, from the milkweed plant. It is a response to a chemical stimulus, a chemotropism or instinctive act.

When disturbed, many plant-eating beetles drop to the ground and remain immovable and by so doing, escape detection. To believe that such insects consciously "feign death" in order to benefit from the act would be tantamount to saying that it is a premeditated and voluntary act and that they know what they are doing. It is more probable that the act is entirely instinctive, albeit a most advantageous one.

Whether insects show any degree of intelligence is a debatable point. Like instinct, it is much a matter of how we define the word intelligence, and, like instinct, it admits of several interpretations. Although instinct is doubtless the underlying force of most insect behavior, can it explain or account for all insect actions? How, for instance, does a bee or wasp leaving the nest for the first time find its way back? Can we explain such behavior on the ground that insects have a mysterious sense of direction? Or do they make use of recognition marks? Wasps, on leaving the nest for the first time, have been observed to make circling flights, which are called orientation flights or location studies, before taking off on a longer flight away from the nest. It is believed that on such flights the wasps memorize certain landmarks to guide them back home, a belief strengthened by the fact that if certain landmarks like stones and weeds are removed or displaced or other objects added, the wasps are unable to find their way back to the nest. We cannot be sure, however, that such actions indicate a degree of intelligence; they may be merely tropic responses. What we once believed to be acts of intelligence, like one ant's recognizing another member of the same community, have since been shown to be reactions to certain stimuli.

If the ability to choose between alternatives is a criterion of intelligence, can we on this basis ascribe a certain amount of intelligence to insects? For they are able to exercise some control over locomotion, to be selective in regard to prey, and to find means to avoid their enemies. All this is the result of experience and would seem to indicate that they have some powers of discrimination. It has been shown that ants can profit by experience and that they have memory in the general sense of the word, but it has also been shown that they have memory images only as a result of sensory stimulation. They are, however, unable to recall certain acts or memory images at will and thus are incapable of reasoning or understanding. Intelligent as they may seem to be in some respects, the social insects show no evidence of abstract reasoning. Even ants are exceedingly stupid in the face of emergencies from which they could extricate themselves by the simplest kind of abstract reasoning. What all this amounts to is that we are unable to draw any line between instinct and intelligence. Insect behavior is undoubtedly purely instinctive, although the social insects may have some slight degree of intelligence.

Biological Supply Houses

Carolina Biological Supply Company
Burlington, North Carolina 27215

Fisher Scientific Company
4901 West LeMoyne Avenue
Chicago, Illinois 60651

Frey Scientific Company
905 Hickory Lane
Mansfield, Ohio 44905

Nova Scientific Corporation
111 Tucker Street
P.O. Box 500
Burlington, North Carolina 27215

Ward's Natural Science Establishment, Inc.
P.O. Box 1712
Rochester, New York 14603

A CATALOGUE OF
SELECTED DOVER BOOKS
IN ALL FIELDS OF INTEREST

A CATALOGUE OF SELECTED DOVER
BOOKS IN ALL FIELDS OF INTEREST

RACKHAM'S COLOR ILLUSTRATIONS FOR WAGNER'S RING. Rackham's finest mature work—all 64 full-color watercolors in a faithful and lush interpretation of the *Ring*. Full-sized plates on coated stock of the paintings used by opera companies for authentic staging of Wagner. Captions aid in following complete Ring cycle. Introduction. 64 illustrations plus vignettes. 72pp. 8⅝ x 11¼. 23779-6 Pa. $6.00

CONTEMPORARY POLISH POSTERS IN FULL COLOR, edited by Joseph Czestochowski. 46 full-color examples of brilliant school of Polish graphic design, selected from world's first museum (near Warsaw) dedicated to poster art. Posters on circuses, films, plays, concerts all show cosmopolitan influences, free imagination. Introduction. 48pp. 9⅜ x 12¼. 23780-X Pa. $6.00

GRAPHIC WORKS OF EDVARD MUNCH, Edvard Munch. 90 haunting, evocative prints by first major Expressionist artist and one of the greatest graphic artists of his time: *The Scream, Anxiety, Death Chamber, The Kiss, Madonna*, etc. Introduction by Alfred Werner. 90pp. 9 x 12. 23765-6 Pa. $5.00

THE GOLDEN AGE OF THE POSTER, Hayward and Blanche Cirker. 70 extraordinary posters in full colors, from Maitres de l'Affiche, Mucha, Lautrec, Bradley, Cheret, Beardsley, many others. Total of 78pp. 9⅜ x 12¼. 22753-7 Pa. $5.95

THE NOTEBOOKS OF LEONARDO DA VINCI, edited by J. P. Richter. Extracts from manuscripts reveal great genius; on painting, sculpture, anatomy, sciences, geography, etc. Both Italian and English. 186 ms. pages reproduced, plus 500 additional drawings, including studies for *Last Supper*, Sforza monument, etc. 860pp. 7⅞ x 10¾. (Available in U.S. only) 22572-0, 22573-9 Pa., Two-vol. set $15.90

THE CODEX NUTTALL, as first edited by Zelia Nuttall. Only inexpensive edition, in full color, of a pre-Columbian Mexican (Mixtec) book. 88 color plates show kings, gods, heroes, temples, sacrifices. New explanatory, historical introduction by Arthur G. Miller. 96pp. 11⅜ x 8½. (Available in U.S. only) 23168-2 Pa. $7.95

UNE SEMAINE DE BONTÉ, A SURREALISTIC NOVEL IN COLLAGE, Max Ernst. Masterpiece created out of 19th-century periodical illustrations, explores worlds of terror and surprise. Some consider this Ernst's greatest work. 208pp. 8⅛ x 11. 23252-2 Pa. $6.00

DRAWINGS OF WILLIAM BLAKE, William Blake. 92 plates from Book of Job, *Divine Comedy, Paradise Lost,* visionary heads, mythological figures, Laocoon, etc. Selection, introduction, commentary by Sir Geoffrey Keynes. 178pp. 8⅛ x 11. 22303-5 Pa. $4.00

ENGRAVINGS OF HOGARTH, William Hogarth. 101 of Hogarth's greatest works: *Rake's Progress, Harlot's Progress, Illustrations for Hudibras, Before and After, Beer Street and Gin Lane,* many more. Full commentary. 256pp. 11 x 13¾. 22479-1 Pa. $12.95

DAUMIER: 120 GREAT LITHOGRAPHS, Honore Daumier. Wide-ranging collection of lithographs by the greatest caricaturist of the 19th century. Concentrates on eternally popular series on lawyers, on married life, on liberated women, etc. Selection, introduction, and notes on plates by Charles F. Ramus. Total of 158pp. 9⅜ x 12¼. 23512-2 Pa. $6.00

DRAWINGS OF MUCHA, Alphonse Maria Mucha. Work reveals draftsman of highest caliber: studies for famous posters and paintings, renderings for book illustrations and ads, etc. 70 works, 9 in color; including 6 items not drawings. Introduction. List of illustrations. 72pp. 9⅜ x 12¼. (Available in U.S. only) 23672-2 Pa. $4.00

GIOVANNI BATTISTA PIRANESI: DRAWINGS IN THE PIERPONT MORGAN LIBRARY, Giovanni Battista Piranesi. For first time ever all of Morgan Library's collection, world's largest. 167 illustrations of rare Piranesi drawings—archeological, architectural, decorative and visionary. Essay, detailed list of drawings, chronology, captions. Edited by Felice Stampfle. 144pp. 9⅜ x 12¼. 23714-1 Pa. $7.50

NEW YORK ETCHINGS (1905-1949), John Sloan. All of important American artist's N.Y. life etchings. 67 works include some of his best art; also lively historical record—Greenwich Village, tenement scenes. Edited by Sloan's widow. Introduction and captions. 79pp. 8⅜ x 11¼. 23651-X Pa. $4.00

CHINESE PAINTING AND CALLIGRAPHY: A PICTORIAL SURVEY, Wan-go Weng. 69 fine examples from John M. Crawford's matchless private collection: landscapes, birds, flowers, human figures, etc., plus calligraphy. Every basic form included: hanging scrolls, handscrolls, album leaves, fans, etc. 109 illustrations. Introduction. Captions. 192pp. 8⅞ x 11¾. 23707-9 Pa. $7.95

DRAWINGS OF REMBRANDT, edited by Seymour Slive. Updated Lippmann, Hofstede de Groot edition, with definitive scholarly apparatus. All portraits, biblical sketches, landscapes, nudes, Oriental figures, classical studies, together with selection of work by followers. 550 illustrations. Total of 630pp. 9⅛ x 12¼. 21485-0, 21486-9 Pa., Two-vol. set $15.00

THE DISASTERS OF WAR, Francisco Goya. 83 etchings record horrors of Napoleonic wars in Spain and war in general. Reprint of 1st edition, plus 3 additional plates. Introduction by Philip Hofer. 97pp. 9⅜ x 8¼. 21872-4 Pa. $4.00

THE EARLY WORK OF AUBREY BEARDSLEY, Aubrey Beardsley. 157 plates, 2 in color: *Manon Lescaut, Madame Bovary, Morte Darthur, Salome,* other. Introduction by H. Marillier. 182pp. 8⅛ x 11. 21816-3 Pa. $4.50

THE LATER WORK OF AUBREY BEARDSLEY, Aubrey Beardsley. Exotic masterpieces of full maturity: *Venus and Tannhauser, Lysistrata, Rape of the Lock, Volpone,* Savoy material, etc. 174 plates, 2 in color. 186pp. 8⅛ x 11. 21817-1 Pa. $5.95

THOMAS NAST'S CHRISTMAS DRAWINGS, Thomas Nast. Almost all Christmas drawings by creator of image of Santa Claus as we know it, and one of America's foremost illustrators and political cartoonists. 66 illustrations. 3 illustrations in color on covers. 96pp. 8⅜ x 11¼. 23660-9 Pa. $3.50

THE DORÉ ILLUSTRATIONS FOR DANTE'S DIVINE COMEDY, Gustave Doré. All 135 plates from Inferno, Purgatory, Paradise; fantastic tortures, infernal landscapes, celestial wonders. Each plate with appropriate (translated) verses. 141pp. 9 x 12. 23231-X Pa. $4.50

DORÉ'S ILLUSTRATIONS FOR RABELAIS, Gustave Doré. 252 striking illustrations of *Gargantua and Pantagruel* books by foremost 19th-century illustrator. Including 60 plates, 192 delightful smaller illustrations. 153pp. 9 x 12. 23656-0 Pa. $5.00

LONDON: A PILGRIMAGE, Gustave Doré, Blanchard Jerrold. Squalor, riches, misery, beauty of mid-Victorian metropolis; 55 wonderful plates, 125 other illustrations, full social, cultural text by Jerrold. 191pp. of text. 9⅜ x 12¼. 22306-X Pa. $7.00

THE RIME OF THE ANCIENT MARINER, Gustave Doré, S. T. Coleridge. Dore's finest work, 34 plates capture moods, subtleties of poem. Full text. Introduction by Millicent Rose. 77pp. 9¼ x 12. 22305-1 Pa. $3.50

THE DORE BIBLE ILLUSTRATIONS, Gustave Doré. All wonderful, detailed plates: Adam and Eve, Flood, Babylon, Life of Jesus, etc. Brief King James text with each plate. Introduction by Millicent Rose. 241 plates. 241pp. 9 x 12. 23004-X Pa. $6.00

THE COMPLETE ENGRAVINGS, ETCHINGS AND DRYPOINTS OF ALBRECHT DURER. "Knight, Death and Devil"; "Melencolia," and more—all Dürer's known works in all three media, including 6 works formerly attributed to him. 120 plates. 235pp. 8⅜ x 11¼. 22851-7 Pa. $6.50

MECHANICK EXERCISES ON THE WHOLE ART OF PRINTING, Joseph Moxon. First complete book (1683-4) ever written about typography, a compendium of everything known about printing at the latter part of 17th century. Reprint of 2nd (1962) Oxford Univ. Press edition. 74 illustrations. Total of 550pp. 6⅛ x 9¼. 23617-X Pa. $7.95

THE COMPLETE WOODCUTS OF ALBRECHT DURER, edited by Dr. W. Kurth. 346 in all: "Old Testament," "St. Jerome," "Passion," "Life of Virgin," Apocalypse," many others. Introduction by Campbell Dodgson. 285pp. 8½ x 12¼. 21097-9 Pa. $7.50

DRAWINGS OF ALBRECHT DURER, edited by Heinrich Wolfflin. 81 plates show development from youth to full style. Many favorites; many new. Introduction by Alfred Werner. 96pp. 8⅛ x 11. 22352-3 Pa. $5.00

THE HUMAN FIGURE, Albrecht Dürer. Experiments in various techniques—stereometric, progressive proportional, and others. Also life studies that rank among finest ever done. Complete reprinting of *Dresden Sketchbook*. 170 plates. 355pp. 8⅜ x 11¼. 21042-1 Pa. $7.95

OF THE JUST SHAPING OF LETTERS, Albrecht Dürer. Renaissance artist explains design of Roman majuscules by geometry, also Gothic lower and capitals. Grolier Club edition. 43pp. 7⅞ x 10¾ 21306-4 Pa. $3.00

TEN BOOKS ON ARCHITECTURE, Vitruvius. The most important book ever written on architecture. Early Roman aesthetics, technology, classical orders, site selection, all other aspects. Stands behind everything since. Morgan translation. 331pp. 5⅜ x 8½. 20645-9 Pa. $4.50

THE FOUR BOOKS OF ARCHITECTURE, Andrea Palladio. 16th-century classic responsible for Palladian movement and style. Covers classical architectural remains, Renaissance revivals, classical orders, etc. 1738 Ware English edition. Introduction by A. Placzek. 216 plates. 110pp. of text. 9½ x 12¾. 21308-0 Pa. $10.00

HORIZONS, Norman Bel Geddes. Great industrialist stage designer, "father of streamlining," on application of aesthetics to transportation, amusement, architecture, etc. 1932 prophetic account; function, theory, specific projects. 222 illustrations. 312pp. 7⅞ x 10¾. 23514-9 Pa. $6.95

FRANK LLOYD WRIGHT'S FALLINGWATER, Donald Hoffmann. Full, illustrated story of conception and building of Wright's masterwork at Bear Run, Pa. 100 photographs of site, construction, and details of completed structure. 112pp. 9¼ x 10. 23671-4 Pa. $5.50

THE ELEMENTS OF DRAWING, John Ruskin. Timeless classic by great Viltorian; starts with basic ideas, works through more difficult. Many practical exercises. 48 illustrations. Introduction by Lawrence Campbell. 228pp. 5⅜ x 8½. 22730-8 Pa. $3.75

GIST OF ART, John Sloan. Greatest modern American teacher, Art Students League, offers innumerable hints, instructions, guided comments to help you in painting. Not a formal course. 46 illustrations. Introduction by Helen Sloan. 200pp. 5⅜ x 8½. 23435-5 Pa. $4.00

THE ANATOMY OF THE HORSE, George Stubbs. Often considered the great masterpiece of animal anatomy. Full reproduction of 1766 edition, plus prospectus; original text and modernized text. 36 plates. Introduction by Eleanor Garvey. 121pp. 11 x 14¾. 23402-9 Pa. $6.00

BRIDGMAN'S LIFE DRAWING, George B. Bridgman. More than 500 illustrative drawings and text teach you to abstract the body into its major masses, use light and shade, proportion; as well as specific areas of anatomy, of which Bridgman is master. 192pp. 6½ x 9¼. (Available in U.S. only) 22710-3 Pa. $3.50

ART NOUVEAU DESIGNS IN COLOR, Alphonse Mucha, Maurice Verneuil, Georges Auriol. Full-color reproduction of *Combinaisons ornementales* (c. 1900) by Art Nouveau masters. Floral, animal, geometric, interlacings, swashes—borders, frames, spots—all incredibly beautiful. 60 plates, hundreds of designs. 9⅜ x 8-1/16. 22885-1 Pa. $4.00

FULL-COLOR FLORAL DESIGNS IN THE ART NOUVEAU STYLE, E. A. Seguy. 166 motifs, on 40 plates, from *Les fleurs et leurs applications decoratives* (1902): borders, circular designs, repeats, allovers, "spots." All in authentic Art Nouveau colors. 48pp. 9⅜ x 12¼. 23439-8 Pa. $5.00

A DIDEROT PICTORIAL ENCYCLOPEDIA OF TRADES AND IN- DUSTRY, edited by Charles C. Gillispie. 485 most interesting plates from the great French Encyclopedia of the 18th century show hundreds of working figures, artifacts, process, land and cityscapes; glassmaking, paper- making, metal extraction, construction, weaving, making furniture, clothing, wigs, dozens of other activities. Plates fully explained. 920pp. 9 x 12. 22284-5, 22285-3 Clothbd., Two-vol. set $40.00

HANDBOOK OF EARLY ADVERTISING ART, Clarence P. Hornung. Largest collection of copyright-free early and antique advertising art ever compiled. Over 6,000 illustrations, from Franklin's time to the 1890's for special effects, novelty. Valuable source, almost inexhaustible.
Pictorial Volume. Agriculture, the zodiac, animals, autos, birds, Christmas, fire engines, flowers, trees, musical instruments, ships, games and sports, much more. Arranged by subject matter and use. 237 plates. 288pp. 9 x 12. 20122-8 Clothbd. $14.50

Typographical Volume. Roman and Gothic faces ranging from 10 point to 300 point, "Barnum," German and Old English faces, script, logotypes, scrolls and flourishes, 1115 ornamental initials, 67 complete alphabets, more. 310 plates. 320pp. 9 x 12. 20123-6 Clothbd. $15.00

CALLIGRAPHY (CALLIGRAPHIA LATINA), J. G. Schwandner. High point of 18th-century ornamental calligraphy. Very ornate initials, scrolls, borders, cherubs, birds, lettered examples. 172pp. 9 x 13. 20475-8 Pa. $7.00

ART FORMS IN NATURE, Ernst Haeckel. Multitude of strangely beautiful natural forms: Radiolaria, Foraminifera, jellyfishes, fungi, turtles, bats, etc. All 100 plates of the 19th-century evolutionist's *Kunstformen der Natur* (1904). 100pp. 9⅜ x 12¼. 22987-4 Pa. $5.00

CHILDREN: A PICTORIAL ARCHIVE FROM NINETEENTH-CENTURY SOURCES, edited by Carol Belanger Grafton. 242 rare, copyright-free wood engravings for artists and designers. Widest such selection available. All illustrations in line. 119pp. 8⅜ x 11¼. 23694-3 Pa. $4.00

WOMEN: A PICTORIAL ARCHIVE FROM NINETEENTH-CENTURY SOURCES, edited by Jim Harter. 391 copyright-free wood engravings for artists and designers selected from rare periodicals. Most extensive such collection available. All illustrations in line. 128pp. 9 x 12. 23703-6 Pa. $4.50

ARABIC ART IN COLOR, Prisse d'Avennes. From the greatest ornamentalists of all time—50 plates in color, rarely seen outside the Near East, rich in suggestion and stimulus. Includes 4 plates on covers. 46pp. 9⅜ x 12¼. 23658-7 Pa. $6.00

AUTHENTIC ALGERIAN CARPET DESIGNS AND MOTIFS, edited by June Beveridge. Algerian carpets are world famous. Dozens of geometrical motifs are charted on grids, color-coded, for weavers, needleworkers, craftsmen, designers. 53 illustrations plus 4 in color. 48pp. 8¼ x 11. (Available in U.S. only) 23650-1 Pa. $1.75

DICTIONARY OF AMERICAN PORTRAITS, edited by Hayward and Blanche Cirker. 4000 important Americans, earliest times to 1905, mostly in clear line. Politicians, writers, soldiers, scientists, inventors, industrialists, Indians, Blacks, women, outlaws, etc. Identificatory information. 756pp. 9¼ x 12¾. 21823-6 Clothbd. $40.00

HOW THE OTHER HALF LIVES, Jacob A. Riis. Journalistic record of filth, degradation, upward drive in New York immigrant slums, shops, around 1900. New edition includes 100 original Riis photos, monuments of early photography. 233pp. 10 x 7⅞. 22012-5 Pa. $7.00

NEW YORK IN THE THIRTIES, Berenice Abbott. Noted photographer's fascinating study of city shows new buildings that have become famous and old sights that have disappeared forever. Insightful commentary. 97 photographs. 97pp. 11⅜ x 10. 22967-X Pa. $5.00

MEN AT WORK, Lewis W. Hine. Famous photographic studies of construction workers, railroad men, factory workers and coal miners. New supplement of 18 photos on Empire State building construction. New introduction by Jonathan L. Doherty. Total of 69 photos. 63pp. 8 x 10¾. 23475-4 Pa. $3.00

THE DEPRESSION YEARS AS PHOTOGRAPHED BY ARTHUR ROTH-STEIN, Arthur Rothstein. First collection devoted entirely to the work of outstanding 1930s photographer: famous dust storm photo, ragged children, unemployed, etc. 120 photographs. Captions. 119pp. 9¼ x 10¾.
23590-4 Pa. $5.00

CAMERA WORK: A PICTORIAL GUIDE, Alfred Stieglitz. All 559 illustrations and plates from the most important periodical in the history of art photography, Camera Work (1903-17). Presented four to a page, reduced in size but still clear, in strict chronological order, with complete captions. Three indexes. Glossary. Bibliography. 176pp. 8⅜ x 11¼.
23591-2 Pa. $6.95

ALVIN LANGDON COBURN, PHOTOGRAPHER, Alvin L. Coburn. Revealing autobiography by one of greatest photographers of 20th century gives insider's version of Photo-Secession, plus comments on his own work. 77 photographs by Coburn. Edited by Helmut and Alison Gernsheim. 160pp. 8⅛ x 11.
23685-4 Pa. $6.00

NEW YORK IN THE FORTIES, Andreas Feininger. 162 brilliant photographs by the well-known photographer, formerly with Life magazine, show commuters, shoppers, Times Square at night, Harlem nightclub, Lower East Side, etc. Introduction and full captions by John von Hartz. 181pp. 9¼ x 10¾.
23585-8 Pa. $6.95

GREAT NEWS PHOTOS AND THE STORIES BEHIND THEM, John Faber. Dramatic volume of 140 great news photos, 1855 through 1976, and revealing stories behind them, with both historical and technical information. Hindenburg disaster, shooting of Oswald, nomination of Jimmy Carter, etc. 160pp. 8¼ x 11.
23667-6 Pa. $5.00

THE ART OF THE CINEMATOGRAPHER, Leonard Maltin. Survey of American cinematography history and anecdotal interviews with 5 masters—Arthur Miller, Hal Mohr, Hal Rosson, Lucien Ballard, and Conrad Hall. Very large selection of behind-the-scenes production photos. 105 photographs. Filmographies. Index. Originally Behind the Camera. 144pp. 8¼ x 11.
23686-2 Pa. $5.00

DESIGNS FOR THE THREE-CORNERED HAT (LE TRICORNE), Pablo Picasso. 32 fabulously rare drawings—including 31 color illustrations of costumes and accessories—for 1919 production of famous ballet. Edited by Parmenia Migel, who has written new introduction. 48pp. 9⅜ x 12¼. (Available in U.S. only)
23709-5 Pa. $5.00

NOTES OF A FILM DIRECTOR, Sergei Eisenstein. Greatest Russian filmmaker explains montage, making of Alexander Nevsky, aesthetics; comments on self, associates, great rivals (Chaplin), similar material. 78 illustrations. 240pp. 5⅜ x 8½.
22392-2 Pa. $4.50

HOLLYWOOD GLAMOUR PORTRAITS, edited by John Kobal. 145 photos capture the stars from 1926-49, the high point in portrait photography. Gable, Harlow, Bogart, Bacall, Hedy Lamarr, Marlene Dietrich, Robert Montgomery, Marlon Brando, Veronica Lake; 94 stars in all. Full background on photographers, technical aspects, much more. Total of 160pp. 8⅜ x 11¼. 23352-9 Pa. $6.00

THE NEW YORK STAGE: FAMOUS PRODUCTIONS IN PHOTO-GRAPHS, edited by Stanley Appelbaum. 148 photographs from Museum of City of New York show 142 plays, 1883-1939. *Peter Pan, The Front Page, Dead End, Our Town,* O'Neill, hundreds of actors and actresses, etc. Full indexes. 154pp. 9½ x 10. 23241-7 Pa. $6.00

DIALOGUES CONCERNING TWO NEW SCIENCES, Galileo Galilei. Encompassing 30 years of experiment and thought, these dialogues deal with geometric demonstrations of fracture of solid bodies, cohesion, leverage, speed of light and sound, pendulums, falling bodies, accelerated motion, etc. 300pp. 5⅜ x 8½. 60099-8 Pa. $4.00

THE GREAT OPERA STARS IN HISTORIC PHOTOGRAPHS, edited by James Camner. 343 portraits from the 1850s to the 1940s: Tamburini, Mario, Caliapin, Jeritza, Melchior, Melba, Patti, Pinza, Schipa, Caruso, Farrar, Steber, Gobbi, and many more—270 performers in all. Index. 199pp. 8⅜ x 11¼. 23575-0 Pa. $7.50

J. S. BACH, Albert Schweitzer. Great full-length study of Bach, life, background to music, music, by foremost modern scholar. Ernest Newman translation. 650 musical examples. Total of 928pp. 5⅜ x 8½. (Available in U.S. only) 21631-4, 21632-2 Pa., Two-vol. set $11.00

COMPLETE PIANO SONATAS, Ludwig van Beethoven. All sonatas in the fine Schenker edition, with fingering, analytical material. One of best modern editions. Total of 615pp. 9 x 12. (Available in U.S. only) 23134-8, 23135-6 Pa., Two-vol. set $15.50

KEYBOARD MUSIC, J. S. Bach. Bach-Gesellschaft edition. For harpsichord, piano, other keyboard instruments. English Suites, French Suites, Six Partitas, Goldberg Variations, Two-Part Inventions, Three-Part Sinfonias. 312pp. 8⅛ x 11. (Available in U.S. only) 22360-4 Pa. $6.95

FOUR SYMPHONIES IN FULL SCORE, Franz Schubert. Schubert's four most popular symphonies: No. 4 in C Minor ("Tragic"); No. 5 in B-flat Major; No. 8 in B Minor ("Unfinished"); No. 9 in C Major ("Great"). Breitkopf & Hartel edition. Study score. 261pp. 9⅜ x 12¼. 23681-1 Pa. $6.50

THE AUTHENTIC GILBERT & SULLIVAN SONGBOOK, W. S. Gilbert, A. S. Sullivan. Largest selection available; 92 songs, uncut, original keys, in piano rendering approved by Sullivan. Favorites and lesser-known fine numbers. Edited with plot synopses by James Spero. 3 illustrations. 399pp. 9 x 12. 23482-7 Pa. $9.95

PRINCIPLES OF ORCHESTRATION, Nikolay Rimsky-Korsakov. Great classical orchestrator provides fundamentals of tonal resonance, progression of parts, voice and orchestra, tutti effects, much else in major document. 330pp. of musical excerpts. 489pp. 6½ x 9¼. 21266-1 Pa. $7.50

TRISTAN UND ISOLDE, Richard Wagner. Full orchestral score with complete instrumentation. Do not confuse with piano reduction. Commentary by Felix Mottl, great Wagnerian conductor and scholar. Study score. 655pp. 8⅛ x 11. 22915-7 Pa. $13.95

REQUIEM IN FULL SCORE, Giuseppe Verdi. Immensely popular with choral groups and music lovers. Republication of edition published by C. F. Peters, Leipzig, n. d. German frontmaker in English translation. Glossary. Text in Latin. Study score. 204pp. 9⅜ x 12¼. 23682-X Pa. $6.00

COMPLETE CHAMBER MUSIC FOR STRINGS, Felix Mendelssohn. All of Mendelssohn's chamber music: Octet, 2 Quintets, 6 Quartets, and Four Pieces for String Quartet. (Nothing with piano is included). Complete works edition (1874-7). Study score. 283 pp. 9⅜ x 12¼. 23679-X Pa. $7.50

POPULAR SONGS OF NINETEENTH-CENTURY AMERICA, edited by Richard Jackson. 64 most important songs: "Old Oaken Bucket," "Arkansas Traveler," "Yellow Rose of Texas," etc. Authentic original sheet music, full introduction and commentaries. 290pp. 9 x 12. 23270-0 Pa. $7.95

COLLECTED PIANO WORKS, Scott Joplin. Edited by Vera Brodsky Lawrence. Practically all of Joplin's piano works—rags, two-steps, marches, waltzes, etc., 51 works in all. Extensive introduction by Rudi Blesh. Total of 345pp. 9 x 12. 23106-2 Pa. $14.95

BASIC PRINCIPLES OF CLASSICAL BALLET, Agrippina Vaganova. Great Russian theoretician, teacher explains methods for teaching classical ballet; incorporates best from French, Italian, Russian schools. 118 illustrations. 175pp. 5⅜ x 8½. 22036-2 Pa. $2.50

CHINESE CHARACTERS, L. Wieger. Rich analysis of 2300 characters according to traditional systems into primitives. Historical-semantic analysis to phonetics (Classical Mandarin) and radicals. 820pp. 6⅛ x 9¼. 21321-8 Pa. $10.00

EGYPTIAN LANGUAGE: EASY LESSONS IN EGYPTIAN HIERO-GLYPHICS, E. A. Wallis Budge. Foremost Egyptologist offers Egyptian grammar, explanation of hieroglyphics, many reading texts, dictionary of symbols. 246pp. 5 x 7½. (Available in U.S. only) 21394-3 Clothbd. $7.50

AN ETYMOLOGICAL DICTIONARY OF MODERN ENGLISH, Ernest Weekley. Richest, fullest work, by foremost British lexicographer. Detailed word histories. Inexhaustible. Do not confuse this with Concise Etymological Dictionary, which is abridged. Total of 856pp. 6½ x 9¼. 21873-2, 21874-0 Pa., Two-vol. set $12.00

A MAYA GRAMMAR, Alfred M. Tozzer. Practical, useful English-language grammar by the Harvard anthropologist who was one of the three greatest American scholars in the area of Maya culture. Phonetics, grammatical processes, syntax, more. 301pp. 5⅜ x 8½.   23465-7 Pa. $4.00

THE JOURNAL OF HENRY D. THOREAU, edited by Bradford Torrey, F. H. Allen. Complete reprinting of 14 volumes, 1837-61, over two million words; the sourcebooks for *Walden*, etc. Definitive. All original sketches, plus 75 photographs. Introduction by Walter Harding. Total of 1804pp. 8½ x 12¼.   20312-3, 20313-1 Clothbd., Two-vol. set $70.00

CLASSIC GHOST STORIES, Charles Dickens and others. 18 wonderful stories you've wanted to reread: "The Monkey's Paw," "The House and the Brain," "The Upper Berth," "The Signalman," "Dracula's Guest," "The Tapestried Chamber," etc. Dickens, Scott, Mary Shelley, Stoker, etc. 330pp. 5⅜ x 8½.   20735-8 Pa. $4.50

SEVEN SCIENCE FICTION NOVELS, H. G. Wells. Full novels. *First Men in the Moon, Island of Dr. Moreau, War of the Worlds, Food of the Gods, Invisible Man, Time Machine, In the Days of the Comet.* A basic science-fiction library. 1015pp. 5⅜ x 8½. (Available in U.S. only)
20264-X Clothbd. $8.95

ARMADALE, Wilkie Collins. Third great mystery novel by the author of *The Woman in White* and *The Moonstone.* Ingeniously plotted narrative shows an exceptional command of character, incident and mood. Original magazine version with 40 illustrations. 597pp. 5⅜ x 8½.
23429-0 Pa. $6.00

MASTERS OF MYSTERY, H. Douglas Thomson. The first book in English (1931) devoted to history and aesthetics of detective story. Poe, Doyle, LeFanu, Dickens, many others, up to 1930. New introduction and notes by E. F. Bleiler. 288pp. 5⅜ x 8½. (Available in U.S. only)
23606-4 Pa. $4.00

FLATLAND, E. A. Abbott. Science-fiction classic explores life of 2-D being in 3-D world. Read also as introduction to thought about hyperspace. Introduction by Banesh Hoffmann. 16 illustrations. 103pp. 5⅜ x 8½.
20001-9 Pa. $2.00

THREE SUPERNATURAL NOVELS OF THE VICTORIAN PERIOD, edited, with an introduction, by E. F. Bleiler. Reprinted complete and unabridged, three great classics of the supernatural: *The Haunted Hotel* by Wilkie Collins, *The Haunted House at Latchford* by Mrs. J. H. Riddell, and *The Lost Stradivarious* by J. Meade Falkner. 325pp. 5⅜ x 8½.
22571-2 Pa. $4.00

AYESHA: THE RETURN OF "SHE," H. Rider Haggard. Virtuoso sequel featuring the great mythic creation, Ayesha, in an adventure that is fully as good as the first book, *She.* Original magazine version, with 47 original illustrations by Maurice Greiffenhagen. 189pp. 6½ x 9¼.
23649-8 Pa. $3.50

UNCLE SILAS, J. Sheridan LeFanu. Victorian Gothic mystery novel, considered by many best of period, even better than Collins or Dickens. Wonderful psychological terror. Introduction by Frederick Shroyer. 436pp. 5⅜ x 8½. 21715-9 Pa. $6.00

JURGEN, James Branch Cabell. The great erotic fantasy of the 1920's that delighted thousands, shocked thousands more. Full final text, Lane edition with 13 plates by Frank Pape. 346pp. 5⅜ x 8½. 23507-6 Pa. $4.50

THE CLAVERINGS, Anthony Trollope. Major novel, chronicling aspects of British Victorian society, personalities. Reprint of Cornhill serialization, 16 plates by M. Edwards; first reprint of full text. Introduction by Norman Donaldson. 412pp. 5⅜ x 8½. 23464-9 Pa. $5.00

KEPT IN THE DARK, Anthony Trollope. Unusual short novel about Victorian morality and abnormal psychology by the great English author. Probably the first American publication. Frontispiece by Sir John Millais. 92pp. 6½ x 9¼. 23609-9 Pa. $2.50

RALPH THE HEIR, Anthony Trollope. Forgotten tale of illegitimacy, inheritance. Master novel of Trollope's later years. Victorian country estates, clubs, Parliament, fox hunting, world of fully realized characters. Reprint of 1871 edition. 12 illustrations by F. A. Faser. 434pp. of text. 5⅜ x 8½. 23642-0 Pa. $5.00

YEKL and THE IMPORTED BRIDEGROOM AND OTHER STORIES OF THE NEW YORK GHETTO, Abraham Cahan. Film *Hester Street* based on *Yekl* (1896). Novel, other stories among first about Jewish immigrants of N.Y.'s East Side. Highly praised by W. D. Howells—Cahan "a new star of realism." New introduction by Bernard G. Richards. 240pp. 5⅜ x 8½. 22427-9 Pa. $3.50

THE HIGH PLACE, James Branch Cabell. Great fantasy writer's enchanting comedy of disenchantment set in 18th-century France. Considered by some critics to be even better than his famous *Jurgen*. 10 illustrations and numerous vignettes by noted fantasy artist Frank C. Pape. 320pp. 5⅜ x 8½. 23670-6 Pa. $4.00

ALICE'S ADVENTURES UNDER GROUND, Lewis Carroll. Facsimile of ms. Carroll gave Alice Liddell in 1864. Different in many ways from final Alice. Handlettered, illustrated by Carroll. Introduction by Martin Gardner. 128pp. 5⅜ x 8½. 21482-6 Pa. $2.50

FAVORITE ANDREW LANG FAIRY TALE BOOKS IN MANY COLORS, Andrew Lang. The four Lang favorites in a boxed set—the complete *Red, Green, Yellow* and *Blue* Fairy Books. 164 stories; 439 illustrations by Lancelot Speed, Henry Ford and G. P. Jacomb Hood. Total of about 1500pp. 5⅜ x 8½. 23407-X Boxed set, Pa. $15.95

HOUSEHOLD STORIES BY THE BROTHERS GRIMM. All the great Grimm stories: "Rumpelstiltskin," "Snow White," "Hansel and Gretel," etc., with 114 illustrations by Walter Crane. 269pp. 5⅜ x 8½.
21080-4 Pa. $3.50

SLEEPING BEAUTY, illustrated by Arthur Rackham. Perhaps the fullest, most delightful version ever, told by C. S. Evans. Rackham's best work. 49 illustrations. 110pp. 7⅞ x 10¾. 22756-1 Pa. $2.50

AMERICAN FAIRY TALES, L. Frank Baum. Young cowboy lassoes Father Time; dummy in Mr. Floman's department store window comes to life; and 10 other fairy tales. 41 illustrations by N. P. Hall, Harry Kennedy, Ike Morgan, and Ralph Gardner. 209pp. 5⅜ x 8½. 23643-9 Pa. $3.00

THE WONDERFUL WIZARD OF OZ, L. Frank Baum. Facsimile in full color of America's finest children's classic. Introduction by Martin Gardner. 143 illustrations by W. W. Denslow. 267pp. 5⅜ x 8½.
20691-2 Pa. $3.50

THE TALE OF PETER RABBIT, Beatrix Potter. The inimitable Peter's terrifying adventure in Mr. McGregor's garden, with all 27 wonderful, full-color Potter illustrations. 55pp. 4¼ x 5½. (Available in U.S. only)
22827-4 Pa. $1.25

THE STORY OF KING ARTHUR AND HIS KNIGHTS, Howard Pyle. Finest children's version of life of King Arthur. 48 illustrations by Pyle. 131pp. 6⅛ x 9¼. 21445-1 Pa. $4.95

CARUSO'S CARICATURES, Enrico Caruso. Great tenor's remarkable caricatures of self, fellow musicians, composers, others. Toscanini, Puccini, Farrar, etc. Impish, cutting, insightful. 473 illustrations. Preface by M. Sisca. 217pp. 8⅜ x 11¼. 23528-9 Pa. $6.95

PERSONAL NARRATIVE OF A PILGRIMAGE TO ALMADINAH AND MECCAH, Richard Burton. Great travel classic by remarkably colorful personality. Burton, disguised as a Moroccan, visited sacred shrines of Islam, narrowly escaping death. Wonderful observations of Islamic life, customs, personalities. 47 illustrations. Total of 959pp. 5⅜ x 8½.
21217-3, 21218-1 Pa., Two-vol. set $12.00

INCIDENTS OF TRAVEL IN YUCATAN, John L. Stephens. Classic (1843) exploration of jungles of Yucatan, looking for evidences of Maya civilization. Travel adventures, Mexican and Indian culture, etc. Total of 669pp. 5⅜ x 8½. 20926-1, 20927-X Pa., Two-vol. set $7.90

AMERICAN LITERARY AUTOGRAPHS FROM WASHINGTON IRVING TO HENRY JAMES, Herbert Cahoon, et al. Letters, poems, manuscripts of Hawthorne, Thoreau, Twain, Alcott, Whitman, 67 other prominent American authors. Reproductions, full transcripts and commentary. Plus checklist of all American Literary Autographs in The Pierpont Morgan Library. Printed on exceptionally high-quality paper. 136 illustrations. 212pp. 9⅛ x 12¼. 23548-3 Pa. $12.50

AN AUTOBIOGRAPHY, Margaret Sanger. Exciting personal account of hard-fought battle for woman's right to birth control, against prejudice, church, law. Foremost feminist document. 504pp. 5⅜ x 8½.

20470-7 Pa. $5.50

MY BONDAGE AND MY FREEDOM, Frederick Douglass. Born as a slave, Douglass became outspoken force in antislavery movement. The best of Douglass's autobiographies. Graphic description of slave life. Introduction by P. Foner. 464pp. 5⅜ x 8½. 22457-0 Pa. $5.50

LIVING MY LIFE, Emma Goldman. Candid, no holds barred account by foremost American anarchist: her own life, anarchist movement, famous contemporaries, ideas and their impact. Struggles and confrontations in America, plus deportation to U.S.S.R. Shocking inside account of persecution of anarchists under Lenin. 13 plates. Total of 944pp. 5⅜ x 8½.

22543-7, 22544-5 Pa., Two-vol. set $12.00

LETTERS AND NOTES ON THE MANNERS, CUSTOMS AND CONDITIONS OF THE NORTH AMERICAN INDIANS, George Catlin. Classic account of life among Plains Indians: ceremonies, hunt, warfare, etc. Dover edition reproduces for first time all original paintings. 312 plates. 572pp. of text. 6⅛ x 9¼. 22118-0, 22119-9 Pa.. Two-vol. set $12.00

THE MAYA AND THEIR NEIGHBORS, edited by Clarence L. Hay, others. Synoptic view of Maya civilization in broadest sense, together with Northern, Southern neighbors. Integrates much background, valuable detail not elsewhere. Prepared by greatest scholars: Kroeber, Morley, Thompson, Spinden, Vaillant, many others. Sometimes called Tozzer Memorial Volume. 60 illustrations, linguistic map. 634pp. 5⅜ x 8½.

23510-6 Pa. $10.00

HANDBOOK OF THE INDIANS OF CALIFORNIA, A. L. Kroeber. Foremost American anthropologist offers complete ethnographic study of each group. Monumental classic. 459 illustrations, maps. 995pp. 5⅜ x 8½.

23368-5 Pa. $13.00

SHAKTI AND SHAKTA, Arthur Avalon. First book to give clear, cohesive analysis of Shakta doctrine, Shakta ritual and Kundalini Shakti (yoga). Important work by one of world's foremost students of Shaktic and Tantric thought. 732pp. 5⅜ x 8½. (Available in U.S. only)

23645-5 Pa. $7.95

AN INTRODUCTION TO THE STUDY OF THE MAYA HIEROGLYPHS, Syvanus Griswold Morley. Classic study by one of the truly great figures in hieroglyph research. Still the best introduction for the student for reading Maya hieroglyphs. New introduction by J. Eric S. Thompson. 117 illustrations. 284pp. 5⅜ x 8½. 23108-9 Pa. $4.00

A STUDY OF MAYA ART, Herbert J. Spinden. Landmark classic interprets Maya symbolism, estimates styles, covers ceramics, architecture, murals, stone carvings as artforms. Still a basic book in area. New introduction by J. Eric Thompson. Over 750 illustrations. 341pp. 8⅜ x 11¼.

21235-1 Pa. $6.95

GEOMETRY, RELATIVITY AND THE FOURTH DIMENSION, Rudolf Rucker. Exposition of fourth dimension, means of visualization, concepts of relativity as Flatland characters continue adventures. Popular, easily followed yet accurate, profound. 141 illustrations. 133pp. 5⅜ x 8½.
23400-2 Pa. $2.75

THE ORIGIN OF LIFE, A. I. Oparin. Modern classic in biochemistry, the first rigorous examination of possible evolution of life from nitrocarbon compounds. Non-technical, easily followed. Total of 295pp. 5⅜ x 8½.
60213-3 Pa. $4.00

PLANETS, STARS AND GALAXIES, A. E. Fanning. Comprehensive introductory survey: the sun, solar system, stars, galaxies, universe, cosmology; quasars, radio stars, etc. 24pp. of photographs. 189pp. 5⅜ x 8½. (Available in U.S. only)
21680-2 Pa. $3.75

THE THIRTEEN BOOKS OF EUCLID'S ELEMENTS, translated with introduction and commentary by Sir Thomas L. Heath. Definitive edition. Textual and linguistic notes, mathematical analysis, 2500 years of critical commentary. Do not confuse with abridged school editions. Total of 1414pp. 5⅜ x 8½.   60088-2, 60089-0, 60090-4 Pa., Three-vol. set $18.50

Prices subject to change without notice.

Available at your book dealer or write for free catalogue to Dept. GI, Dover Publications, Inc., 180 Varick St., N.Y., N.Y. 10014. Dover publishes more than 175 books each year on science, elementary and advanced mathematics, biology, music, art, literary history, social sciences and other areas.

For my brother, Kevin
—C.B.C.

WWW.JURASSICPARK.COM

Jurassic World is a trademark and copyright of Universal
Studios and Amblin Entertainment, Inc. Licensed by
Universal Studios Licensing LLC. All Rights Reserved.

it us on the Web!
pIntoReading.com
domhousekids.com

ucators and librarians, for a variety of teaching tools, visit us at RHTeachersLibrarians.com

N 978-0-553-53687-4 (trade) — ISBN 978-0-553-53688-1 (lib. bdg.) —
N 978-0-553-53689-8 (ebook)

nted in the United States of America
19 18 17 16 15 14 13

Dear Parents:

Congratulations! Your child is taking
the first steps on an exciting journey.
The destination? Independent reading!

STEP INTO READING® will help your child get there. The
five steps to reading success. Each step includes fun storie
art or photographs. In addition to original fiction and book
characters, there are Step into Reading Non-Fiction Reader
and Boxed Sets, Sticker Readers, and Comic Readers—a co
program with something to interest every child.

Learning to Read, Step by Step!

Ready to Read   Preschool–Kindergart
• big type and easy words • rhyme and rhythm • p
For children who know the alphabet and are
begin reading.

Reading with Help   Preschool–Grade
• basic vocabulary • short sentences • simple sto
For children who recognize familiar words a
new words with help.

Reading on Your Own   Grades 1–3
• engaging characters • easy-to-follow plots • po
For children who are ready to read on their o

Reading Paragraphs   Grades 2–3
• challenging vocabulary • short paragraphs • e
For newly independent readers who read sil
with confidence.

Ready for Chapters   Grades 2–4
• chapters • longer paragraphs • full-color art
For children who want to take the plunge in
but still like colorful pictures.

STEP INTO READING® is designed to give every child
reading experience. The grade levels are only guides; ch
through the steps at their own speed, developing confide

Remember, a lifetime love of reading starts with a single